D1274231

CLASSIC
FIGHTER
AIRCRAFT

MARTIN W. BOWMAN

EVANSTON PUBLIC LIBRARY
1703 ORRINGTON AVENUE
EVANSTON, ILLINOIS 60201

Patrick Stephens, Wellingborough

© Martin W. Bowman 1987

All rights reserved. No part of this publication
may be reproduced, stored in a retrieval system or transmitted,
in any form or by any means, electronic, mechanical,
photocopying, recording or otherwise, without prior permission
in writing from Patrick Stephens Limited.

First published in July 1987

British Library Cataloguing in Publication Data

Bowman, Martin W.
Classic fighter aircraft
1. Fighter planes — History
I. Title
623.74'64'09   UG1242.F5

ISBN 0–85059–874–5

Front cover *The F-15 Eagle is a potent air-superiority fighter
with superb aerodynamic and electronic performance* (via
Chris Chant).

Back cover *The classic fighter lines of the P-51 Mustang I are evident in
this example No 2 Squadron RAF, photographed in 1943* (Charles Brown,
RAF Museum).

*Patrick Stephens Limited is part of the
Thorsons Publishing Group*

Printed and bound in Great Britain

CONTENTS

INTRODUCTION

Classic Fighter Aircraft consists of forty-five of the most famous fighter/strike aircraft to have flown since 1914. My choice covers a wide platform and includes: fighters of World War One; biplane fighters of the inter-war years; propeller types and jet designs of the Allied and Axis powers during World War Two; and finally the combat types used since 1945 in NATO, in Korea, Vietnam and the Falklands.

Rudyard Kipling wrote, 'I have five friends good and true. They are what? why? where? when? and who?' In this book the reader will learn what aircraft was the most successful fighter of WWI, the first RAF fighter of all-metal structure, the first US Navy fighter to exceed 400 mph in level flight, and the one to remain in production the longest. What was the first operational interceptor capable of sustained Mach 2+ speeds?

The first USAF and RAF jet fighters are featured but can you name the first operational aircraft to have an ejector seat? Where the first transonic, swept-wing jet fighter of the Western Alliance first saw combat service and what was the first RAF jet to fly the Atlantic? When did a strike fighter establish eight world time-to-height records? When did an aircraft hold World airspeed and altitude records simultaneously? Who designed the fighter responsible for destroying more enemy aircraft by day than any other aircraft in history?

Why are the Focke Wulf 190, Sea Harrier and Super Sabre, to name but a few, missing from this book? The answer is that they will appear in a second in the series along with many other classic, noteworthy and famous fighters which have flown during the past 72 years.

Martin W. Bowman
May 1987

ACKNOWLEDGEMENTS

My thanks to Mike Bailey, Harry Holmes, Hans-Heiri Stapfer and Peter Frost of the Norfolk & Suffolk Aviation Society for their help and kindness in providing me with several photographs for this book. My thanks too to Trevor Deary for his German translations. I am also most grateful to Grumman Aerospace, Rolls-Royce, Lockheed, British Aerospace, General Dynamics and North American for their up to the minute data and photographs on the more modern jet fighters.

ARMSTRONG WHITWORTH SISKIN III/IIIA

Type Day fighter. **Crew** Pilot only. **Manufacturers** Armstrong Whitworth Aircraft, Coventry. Sub-contracted by Blackburn, Bristol, Gloster and Vickers. **Specification (IIIA) — Power plant** One 420–450 hp Armstrong Siddeley Jaguar IV. **Dimensions** Span 33 ft 2 in. Length 25 ft 4 in. Height 10 ft 2 in. **Weight** Empty, 2,061 lb. Loaded, 3,012 lb. **Performance** Max speed, 156 mph at sea level. Service ceiling 27,000 ft. **Armament** Two synchronized Vickers guns. Provision for four 20 lb bombs below wings.
below wings.

The production Siskin III became the first RAF fighter of all-metal structure when it entered service in May 1924 with 41 Squadron at Northolt. With the Gloster Grebe the Siskin III was the first new fighter type to equip the RAF since 1918. Siskin development began in 1918 with the Siddeley Siskin which was of wooden construction. This was fitted with a 340 hp ABC Dragonfly radial engine until the Armstrong-Siddeley Jaguar engine was developed. The Siskin II two-seat trainer flew in the King's Cup air race of 1922. The following year the prototype Siskin flew for the first time. During this period manufactur-

The Armstrong Whitworth Siskin III was powered by a 340 hp ABC Dragonfly radial engine until it was replaced by the more powerful Armstrong Siddeley Jaguar 4, as fitted here.

Armstrong Whitworth Siskin IIIAs of 43 Squadron practise tied-together formation flying for the Hendon Display of 1930 (Flight).

ers were still geared mainly to the wooden construction methods used during the First World War. However, the Mk II trainer had a metal fuselage and wooden wings. It was followed by the Mk II fighter which was similarly constructed.

Some 62 Siskin IIIs were built (including twelve trainers). The more successful Siskin IIIA entered service with III Squadron in September 1926. About 400 were built for the RAF and eleven squadrons eventually operated the type. During 1927–31 brightly painted Siskin IIIAs performed superb aerobatic displays, the most memorable of which was at the Hendon air pageant when 43 Squadron performed tied-together aerobatics in squadron formation. Siskin IIIAs remained in service until 1932.

BRISTOL F2B FIGHTER

Type Fighting-scout. **Crew** Two. **Manufacturers** Bristol Aeroplane Company. **Power Plant** (F2A) One 190 hp Rolls-Royce Falcon I (F2B) One 275 hp Rolls-Royce Falcon III. **Dimensions** Span 39 ft 4 in. Length 25 ft 10 in. Height 9 ft 9 in. **Weight** Empty, 1,745 lb. Loaded, 2,590 lb. **Performance** Max speed, 125 mph at sea level; 108 mph at 13,000 ft. **Armament** One Vickers and one or two Lewis guns. Two 112 lb bombs below wings.

The 'Biff' or 'Brisfit' as it was affectionately known, was designed by Captain Frank Barnwell (RFC) and L. G. Frise and flew for the first time in September 1916. The F2A's fuselage mounted high between the wings gave its pilot an excellent view above and below the top wing and the type was first used in an armed-reconnaissance role.

On 8 March 1917 No 48 Squadron, commanded by Captain Leefe-Robinson VC, flew the first production F2As to France. Used operationally for the first time on 5 April 1917, during the spring offensive on the Western Front, No 48 Squadron suffered early heavy losses as German fighter pilots exploited the type's poor defensive tactics, attacking from below and directly astern. In the autumn of

Bristol F2bs of 141 Squadron at Biggin Hill, Kent in late 1918. These aircraft were intended for home defence but as German raids had by this time ceased, the Squadron was used to test ground-to-air wireless (Norfolk/ Suffolk Aviation Museum).

1917 the Falcon III engine became available and was fitted to the F2B. This type also incorporated several changes, including the deletion of the side radiators, to improve forward view from the cockpit.

The RFC soon learned to use the F2B in an offensive role, for despite its weight and size, the Bristol Fighter was as fast and manoeuvrable as the German single-seat machines and could dive faster than any other type on the Western Front. In a dog-fight the pilot learned to fly it like a single-seater, using his forward firing Vickers gun in the manner of a fighting scout while the observer guarded his rear with single or twin Lewis guns mounted on a Scarff ring. In this role the Brisfit proved a powerful and effective weapon and it developed into the finest two-seat fighter of World War One.

By the end of the war Bristol Fighters equipped fourteen squadrons and some 3,100 had been built. The type saw widespread post-war service as the RAF's standard army-co-operation aircraft in Ireland and Germany until 1922 and on the Northwest Frontier of India and in Iraq until 1932 when they were finally superseded by Fairey Gordons. Bristol Fighters also equipped eight foreign air forces. When production finally ceased in December 1926, a further 1,369 models had been built.

BRISTOL BULLDOG

Type Day and night fighter. **Crew** Pilot only. **Manufacturers** Bristol Aeroplane Co, Filton. **Specification (Bulldog IIA) — Power plant** One 490 hp Bristol Jupiter VIIF or VIIF.P. **Dimensions** Span 33 ft 11 in. Length 25 ft 2 in. Height, 9 ft 10 in. **Weight** Empty, 2,412 lb. Loaded, 3,503 lb. **Performance** Max speed, 174 mph at 10,000 ft. Service ceiling 27,000 ft. **Armament** Twin, synchronized Vickers machine-guns. Four 20 lb bombs.

When the RAF issued a requirement in 1926 for a day and night fighter to succeed the Siskin and Gamecock, the Bulldog emerged victorious after competition with no less than nine other types. The Mk I prototype flew for the first time on 17 May 1927. In June 1929 Bulldogs began equipping 3 Squadron at Upavon. At that time the Bulldog was the last word in fighters but it was not as manoeuvrable as the Gamecock. It was heavier and tended to sink faster on its back in the middle of a slow roll. Low aerobatics in a Bulldog were absolutely

Bristol Bulldog Mk IIs of 17 Squadron in 1929: the second squadron to operate the Bulldog (111 was the first). Some of the 111 Squadron's aircraft were acquired by 17 Squadron and K-1085 and K-1081 still retain the former's green bands on their wings (Flight).

Bristol Bulldog Mk IIA, K-2227, in the colours of 56 Squadron with Gloster Gladiator L8032 of the Shuttleworth Trust behind. K-2227 was written off in a crash in 1964 (Rex Barrett).

forbidden. In July 1931 Bulldogs finally replaced 26 Squadron's Gamecocks, the last unit to operate the type. One 26 Squadron pilot was killed performing low aerobatics and on 14 December 1931 Pilot Officer (later Group Captain) Douglas Bader lost both his legs as a result of an air crash while performing aerobatics in a Bulldog.

By 1932 Bulldogs equipped nine RAF squadrons at home and abroad. The last of the Bulldogs in Home Defence squadrons, which constituted some 70 per cent of the UK fighting defence for some years, were finally replaced by Gladiators in 1937. Altogether, 312 Bulldogs were built for the RAF, the first 48 being designated Mk II and the remainder, Mk IIA. The later marks had a redesigned oil system, increased weight and strengthened structure.

The Bulldog will always be remembered for its colourful and thrilling aerobatic displays at Hendon from 1929–36. And although it never saw action with the RAF the Bulldog fought with some distinction on the side of the Finns against Russia during the Winter War of 1939–40.

BRISTOL BEAUFIGHTER

Type Torpedo strike fighter and night fighter. **Crew** Two. **Manufacturers** Bristol Aeroplane Company, Filton and Weston-super-Mare. **Power plant** Two 1,770 hp Bristol Hercules XVII. **Dimensions** Span, 57 ft 10 in. Length, 41 ft 8 in. Height, 15 ft 10 in. **Weight** Empty, 15,600 lb. Loaded, 25,400 lb. **Performance** Max speed, 330 mph. Service ceiling, 30,000 ft. Range, 1,540 miles. **Armament** Four 20 mm Hispano cannon fixed in underside or forward of the fuselage and one .303 in Vickers K machine-gun mounted in observer's compartment firing aft (fighters, also six .303 in Brownings, two fixed in outer port wing and four in right). One 1,605 lb torpedo on centre line or two 2,127 lb and wing racks for eight rocket projectiles or two 1,000 lb bombs.

Bristol's chief designer Leslie Frise and engine designer Roy Fedden sought to create a twin-engined, cannon-armed fighter by combining all that was best in the Blenheim and Beaufort. Fedden proposed using the wings, tail unit and undercarriage of the Beaufort combined with a redesigned forward fuselage and up-rated engines. Design of this private venture began in 1938 and the Type 156 prototype flew for the first time on 17 July 1939.

Using Beaufort construction methods enabled the Beaufighter to be built quickly and the Air Ministry, realizing its potential, ordered 300 production models. Evaluation trials commenced in April 1940 but the low-power Hercules engines proved a disappointment. On take-off and landing it tended to swing and also to be longitudinally unstable at low speeds. This was partially rectified on the Beaufighter IIF by adding a large dorsal fin and dihedral tailplane. It had been planned to fit Rolls-Royce Griffon engines in the IIF but the Fairey Firefly took priority. The Stirling bomber captured a large share of the Hercules market so less powerful Rolls Royce Merlin XX engines were fitted instead to all 450 Beaufighter IIFs.

The first Beaufighters entered squadron service in September 1940 and played a leading role as a night fighter during the Blitz. On 19 November 1940 the first enemy aircraft destroyed at night by a Beaufighter using A1 Mk IV radar, a Junkers Ju 88, fell to the guns of a 604 Squadron machine. In March 1941 the Beaufighter began supplanting the Blenheim IVF as the standard long-range fighter of Coastal Command. Gradually, Beaufighters began serving in all theatres, from the Western Desert to the Far East. In May 1941, when over 200 had been delivered to the RAF, Beaufighters began operations from Malta and the Mk IIF entered service with home-based squadrons.

Above *Bristol Beaufighter IC, R2198, B-Baker of 252 Squadron displaying early camouflage markings. Note that wing guns are not fitted on this example (IWM).*

Below *The Beaufighter Mk 10, distinguishable by the thimble nose radio which housed ASB radar, was fitted with underwing racks for eight rocket projectiles in 1945.*

The Mk VI Beaufighter exchanged the Merlin for the Hercules radial and the Mk VIC was fitted with a backwards-firing Vickers K gun in addition to the 'Beau''s normal armament of four 20 mm guns in the nose and six .303 inch guns in the wings. In 1942 Coastal Command Beaufighter VIs were adapted to carry torpedoes and the type became known as the 'Torbeau'. In May 1943 the rocket-firing version of the Mk VIC entered service and this type was sometimes known as the 'Flakbeau'. Coastal Command Beaufighters carried out their first successful operation against enemy shipping on 18 April 1943 but one of their most memorable feats of the war took place much earlier, on 12 June 1942 when a Beaufighter of 236 Squadron, Coastal Command, flew at low level to Paris in broad daylight and released a 'tricouleur' on the Champs-Elysees before raking the Gestapo headquarters with murderous cannon fire.

In September 1942 Beaufighters began equipping squadrons in the Far East, specializing in low-level attacks on airfields and shipping and earning the nickname, 'Whispering death' (a reference to the sound of the Beaufighter's sleeve-valve engines). By 1943 the Beaufighter had all but been replaced in the night fighter role by the Mosquito and deliveries of the Mk X went to Coastal Command. Its most significant feature was a thimble nose radome which housed ASV radar. The Mk X, of which 2,205 were built, packed a hefty punch, being able to carry a combination of bombs, a torpedo and rockets. Altogether, 5,928 Beaufighters were built, including 364 by the Department of Aircraft Production in Australia. Production ceased in September 1945 but the TT10 continued to serve in the Middle and Far East, the last finally being retired on 12 May 1960.

De HAVILLAND MOSQUITO

Type (VI) Fighter-bomber. (II) Night fighter. **Crew** Two. **Manufacturers** de Havilland Aircraft Co Ltd, Hatfield. (VI) Sub-contracted by Airspeed and Standard Motors, Canley. **Specification (Mark VI) — Power plant** Two Rolls-Royce Merlin XXI or Merlin 25. **Dimensions** Span, 54 ft 2 in. Length, 40 ft 6 in. Height, 15 ft 3 in. **Weight** Empty, 14,300 lb. Loaded, 21,600 lb. **Performance** Max speed, 380 mph at 13,000 ft. Range (normal), 1,205 miles. 1,770 with additional fuel tanks. **Armament** (VI, Series 2) Four 20 mm cannon and four .303 in machine-guns in nose. Two 500 lb bombs in bomb bay and two 500 lb bombs below wings.

Had it not been for the determination shown by de Havilland to produce what was, in the late 1930s, a radical and unorthodox design, Britain might never have possessed what is arguably regarded as the finest two-engined fighter-bomber of the Second World War. The Mosquito was to reign supreme as a night fighter, anti-shipping strike and rocket-firing ground support aircraft.

At first the Air Ministry showed no interest in the Mosquito, suggesting instead that de Havilland should concentrate on wing assemblies for proven types. Undismayed, de Havillands began detailed design work in December 1939 on the prototype, built secretly at Salisbury Hall and completed in only eleven months. It was not until 1940 and then mainly because of the interest shown by Air Marshal Sir Wilfred Freeman (the Member for Research, Development and Production on the Air Council) that official backing was received, albeit reluctantly.

On 1 March 1940 the Air Staff issued an order for fifty bombers against Specification B.I/40. De Havilland's original private venture built around two Merlin engines was required to carry a 1,000 lb bomb load for 1,500 miles. However, the threat of invasion after Dunkirk prompted the Ministry of Aircraft Production to concentrate on established aircraft and for a time the 'Wooden Wonder' was low on the list of priorities.

On 25 November 1940 the prototype Mosquito flew for the first time at Hatfield and astounded everyone with a remarkable top speed of almost 400 mph and a display of superb manoeuvrability involving upward rolls with one airscrew feathered. The original contract for fifty bombers was changed to twenty bombers and thirty fighters.

On 15 May 1941 the Mosquito night-fighter prototype flew for the first time and was designated Mosquito II. The type was fitted with the then highly secret AI Mk IV airborne radar device for intercepting

The most widely used of all the Mosquito fighters, the Mk IV was developed as a result of the success gained by the Mosquito II (British Aerospace).

enemy bombers at night. The fighter variant of the Mosquito differed from the bomber variant in having strengthened wing spars to take the extra strain imposed by fighter manoeuvres and the nose was modified to house four 20 mm cannon and four machine-guns. A flat, bullet-proof windscreen was fitted and the two-man crew entered through a door on the starboard side of the fuselage instead of through a hatch in the floor as on the bomber. Several experimental changes were made to the prototype Mosquito II including the trial installations of a mock-up dorsal turret and later, a Turbinlight searchlight in the nose.

The Mosquito II first entered service with Fighter Command in January 1942. Of the 466 Mosquito IIs built, 97 were later converted to Mk XII with improved radar and no nose machine-guns. It was followed by the Mk XIII, which flew for the first time in February 1944. Some 270 were built before production switched to the Mk XIX fitted with Merlin 25 engines and the Mk XXX, introduced in 1944. The Mk XXX was the final night-fighter version of the Mosquito to see wartime service. Mosquito night-fighters successfully defended Great Britain from enemy operations for three years and destroyed 1,200 enemy aircraft and V1s in sixty nights.

The most widely used of all the Mosquito fighters was the Mk VI fighter-bomber which was developed as a result of the success gained by the Mosquito II night-intruder. Altogether, about 2,500 Mk VIs were built. The prototype was a converted Mk II and flew for the first time in February 1943. At first, in addition to their normal defensive armament, they also carried two 250 lb bombs in the rear of the bomb

Mosquito II, DD737, with nose guns. The Mosquito night-fighter was progressively improved, mainly by the introduction of the more efficient A1 radar (British Aerospace).

bay and two more under the wings. The Mk VI first entered service with 418 Squadron, Fighter Command at Holmesley South in May 1943 in the day and night intruder role.

From February 1944 the Mosquito VI began equipping Coastal Command squadrons in the anti-shipping role, fitted with eight 60 lb rocket-projectiles below the wings. In open seas no enemy shipping was safe from the Mosquito's machine-guns and rockets, which when fired as a complete salvo, were equivalent in firepower to a broadside from a 10,000 ton cruiser. The Mosquito XVIII, which was originally named 'Tse-Tse', first entered service with 248 Squadron, Coastal Command in October 1943. It sported a 57 mm Molins gun (equivalent to a six-pounder field gun).

The most memorable operations carried out by Mosquitoes during World War Two were low-level attacks by Mosquito VIs of No 2 Group, 2nd Tactical Air Force. This special detachment, established just

shortly before D-Day, was responsible for three audacious low-level strikes on German targets in occupied-Europe. The first occurred on 18 February 1944 when nineteen Mosquito VIs led by Group Captain P. C. Pickard carried out a daring daylight raid on the prison at Amiens, France. The walls of the prison were breached and as a result, 258 members of the French Resistance were able to escape.

On 11 April 1944 six Mosquito VIs of 613 Squadron destroyed the Kleizkamp Art Galleries in The Hague, which was being used as a depository for Gestapo records of the Dutch Resistance. The most brilliant low-level attack took place on 21 March 1945 when Mosquito fighter-bombers of 464 Squadron destroyed Gestapo records of the Danish Resistance held in Shell House in the centre of Copenhagen. The raid also enabled some members of the Danish resistance, who were being held captive on the sixth floor, to escape.

Post-war the Mosquito served with the RAF both at home and abroad. Principally, the NF 36 and NF 38 night-fighter versions served with Fighter Command until the advent of jet night-fighter aircraft in 1951. The NF 38 was the last Mosquito type to be produced. Altogether, 7,781 Mosquitoes incorporating 43 different operational marks, were built in Britain, Canada and Australia.

De HAVILLAND VAMPIRE

Type (NF 10) Night fighter. (F1) Interceptor fighter. (FB9) Fighter-bomber. **Crew** Pilot only. **Manufacturers** de Havilland Aircraft Co Ltd, Hatfield and Chester. (F1 & FB9) sub-contracted by English Electric, Preston **Power plant** (F1) One 3,100 lb thrust de Havilland Goblin DGn2 (FB9 & NF10) one 3,350 lb thrust Goblin DGn3. **Dimensions** (F1) Span, 40 ft (FB9 & NF10) 38 ft. Length, (F1), 30 ft 9 in (NF10) 34 ft 7 in. Height, (F1) 8 ft 10 in. (NF10), 6 ft 7 in. **Weight** (FB9) Empty, 7,283 lb. Loaded, 12,390 lb. **Performance** (F1) Max speed, 540 mph at 20,000 ft. Range 730 miles. **Armament** (F1 & NF10) four 20 mm cannon in nose. (FB9) four 20 mm cannon and provision for 2,000 lb of bombs or rockets below wings.

At first the aircraft was known as the Spider-Crab, designed to Specification E6/41, the twin-boom configuration being chosen to minimize the length of the jetpipe and thus the power losses. The prototype Vampire flew for the first time at Hatfield in September 1943 powered by a 2,700 lb thrust de Havilland Goblin turbojet. The first fifty F1s were unpressurized but all subsequent models had a pressurized cockpit and the original three-piece canopy was eventually replaced by a bubble hood. The Vampire F1 became the second type of jet fighter to enter service with the RAF when it equipped 247 Squadron in April 1946.

The prototype Vampire FIII flew for the first time on 4 November 1946 and the production models, which differed from the F1 in having increased fuel tankage in the wings and a re-designed tail assembly, superseded the F1 in Fighter Command and in Germany. Some F3s remained in service with the Auxiliary Air Force until as late as 1952. In July 1948 six Vampire F3s from 54 Squadron became the first RAF jets to fly the Atlantic when they flew from England to the USA via refuelling stops at Iceland, Greenland and Labrador.

In 1949 the Vampire FB5 (fighter-bomber) variant appeared in the close-support ground-attack role. It had cut-down wing tips, strengthened skinning and rocket-projectiles. The FB9 was a tropicalized version of the FB5 with an air-conditioned cockpit for operations in the Far and Middle East. Vampire FB9s of 8 Squadron based at Aden took part in operations against the Mau-Mau in Kenya. In 1954–55 the Vampire FB9 was replaced by the Venom FB1 and the FB5 ended its career equipping Flying Training Schools in the UK.

The Vampire night-fighter version began life as a de Havilland private venture known as the DH113 in 1949. It was not originally intended for the RAF, which at this time was operating the Meteor NF11 in this role. The first batch of DH113s were bought by the

One of about 900 de Havilland Vampire FB5s built for the RAF (VV217). This variant was the first jet fighter to operate with the RAF in the Far East, entering service with 60 Squadron at Tengah in December 1950 (British Aerospace).

Egyptian Air Force but when the sale of arms to this country was banned, the RAF took over the remaining DH113s under the designation NF10. These supplemented the Meteor NF11s and speeded up replacement of the night-fighter force which was still largely equipped with Mosquitoes. The Vampire NF10 entered service with 25 Squadron at West Malling, Kent in 1951 and equipped a number of squadrons until it was withdrawn in 1954. Some were later sold to the Indian Air Force and a few remained in service with the RAF as navigator trainers until May 1959.

ENGLISH ELECTRIC LIGHTNING

Type All-weather interceptor. **Crew** Pilot only. **Manufacturers** English Electric Aviation. **Power plant** Two 15,680 lb thrust Rolls-Royce Avon 302 augmented turbojets. **Dimensions** Span 34 ft 10 in. Length 53 ft 3 in. Height 19 ft 7 in. **Weight** Empty, 28,000 lb. Loaded, 50,000 lb. **Performance** Max speed, 1,500 mph at 40,000 ft. Service ceiling, 60,000+ ft. **Armament** Two Red Top or Firestreak guided missiles, or two 30 mm Aden cannon.

The Lightning intereceptor remains one of the most exciting and most powerful aircraft ever to equip the RAF. It is still standard equipment in two RAF interceptor squadrons some 27 years after it first entered service.

Designed by W.E.W. 'Teddy' Petter, designer of the Canberra, the original Sapphire-powered P1 flew for the first time in August 1954 when it exceeded Mach 1. In November 1958 the Avon-powered

The Lightning, developed from the P1 research aircraft, was the first British fighter to fly at twice the speed of sound. This Mk 3 version, XR754, has the enlarged ventral fuel tank.

A pair of BAC Lightning F6s. The nearer aircraft is armed with two HS Red Top missiles of greater performance than the HS Firestreak missiles which arm XP738 *of 111 Squadron* (Hawker Siddeley).

Lightning attained Mach 2 and became the RAF's first single-seat fighter capable of exceeding the speed of sound in level flight. Three P1B prototypes were built, followed by twenty pre-production aircraft which were used for armament, radar and handling trials.

The first production Lightning F1 flew for the first time in October 1959 and the type entered RAF service with the Central Fighter Establishment at Coltishall, Norfolk in December that year. In July 1960 74 Squadron, also at RAF Coltishall, became the first operational unit to be equipped with the F1 and the type became the principal air defence fighter in both Fighter (later Strike) Command and RAF Germany.

In 1963 the F2, with fully variable afterburner, equipped 19 and 92 Squadrons of RAF Fighter Command at Leconfield. Between 1964 and 1968 the major Lightning variant was the F3 which differed principally from earlier marks in having its two Aden nose cannon deleted and carrying a pair of Red Top missiles in place of the earlier Firestreaks. Provision was also made for two over-wing fuel tanks and the fin and rudder were squared off at the tip. The Lightning T4 and T5 are two-seat trainer versions of the F2 and F3 respectively.

In 1965 BAC developed a kinked and cambered wing to improve operation at vastly increased weights, reduce subsonic drag and thus extend the range. This fully developed version of the Lightning was originally known as the F Mk 3A but was later designated the Lightning F Mk 6. Fuel capacity was almost doubled by the installation of an enlarged ventral fuel tank containing 600 gallons. The F6 prototype first flew on 17 April 1964 and first equipped 5 Squadron at Binbrook in November 1965. All Home Defence F3s were subsequently retro-fitted to F6 standard and later equipped Nos 11, 23, 56, 74 and 111 Squadrons in Fighter (later Strike) Command.

By mid-1967 all Lightnings were capable of being refuelled in flight. In August that year the final Lightning was completed on the Preston production line. On 25 April 1968 five operational and one OCU Lightning squadrons led the fly-past over Bentley Priory to mark the disbandment of Fighter Command. From 1974 Lightnings began to be replaced by Phantoms in the Air Defence role and plans to initiate a third Lightning squadron in 1979 were abandoned as an economy measure. However, Nos 5 and 11 Squadrons of the Binbrook Wing (and the Lightning Training Flight) will retain their F Mk 6 Lightnings until replacement by the Tornado F Mk 2. Binbrook currently has 72 Lightning F3s, F6s and T5s (including about forty in storage).

In all 338 Lightnings have been built, including 57 multi-role fighter and attack variants sold to Kuwait and the Royal Saudi Air Force.

FAIREY FLYCATCHER

Type Carrier-borne fighter. **Crew** Pilot only. **Manufacturers** Fairey Aviation, Hayes, Middlesex. **Power plant** One 400 hp Armstrong Siddeley Jaguar III or IV. **Dimensions** Span, 29 ft. Length, 23 ft. Height, 12 ft. **Weight** Empty, 2,039 lb. Loaded, 3,028 lb. **Performance** Max speed, 133 mph at 5,000 ft. 110 mph at 17,000 ft. Service ceiling, 19,000 ft. **Armament** Two synchronized Vickers machine-guns. Provision for four 20 lb bombs below wings.

One of the Royal Navy's classic fleet fighters, this stubby, rugged little machine was for many years the standard first-line fighter in the FAA and the Royal Navy's only Fleet fighter from 1923 until 1932, when the Hawker Nimrod joined it in service. During its career the type was also used as a landplane and as a float plane.

Despite its ungainly appearance, the Flycatcher was a superb aerobatic aircraft and perfect for carrier operations. It had excellent take-off and landing characteristics as a result of adjustable flaps which ran along the entire trailing edges of both wings. These helped

The carrier-borne Fairey Flycatcher was a stubby, rugged little fighter of the inter-war years. This aircraft is N9928 of No 403 Flight (Charles E. Brown).

reduce the long take-off and landing runs normally associated with deck-flying operations.

The Flycatcher served in all the aircraft carriers of the day and was the last Fleet fighter to operate from short take-off platforms mounted on the gun-turrets of capital ships. On 26 November 1929 a Flycatcher from Halfar, Malta, became the first Fleet fighter to make a night landing on a carrier when it alighted on the deck of HMS *Courageous*. In 1934 Flycatchers were entirely replaced by the Nimrod and Osprey in Fleet service.

FOKKER D-VII

Type Fighter. **Crew** Pilot only. **Manufacturers** Fokker Works, Schwerin. Built under licence by Albatros at Johannisthal and Schneidemuhl. **Power plant** BMW IIIa or Mercedes 160 hp engines. **Dimensions** Span, 29 ft 3½ in. Length, 22 ft 9¾ in. Height, 9 ft 2 in. **Weight** Empty, 1,513 lb. Loaded, 1,993 lb. **Performance** Max speed, 124 mph at sea level. Service ceiling, 22,900 ft. **Armament** Two fixed 7.92 mm Spandau machine-guns.

The Fokker D-VII is generally regarded as the finest fighter of the First World War. Anthony Fokker (a Dutchman) and Reinhold Platz's VII design, based on the tri-decker Dr I, won the single-seat fighter competition in January 1918. Extremely manoeuvrable at high altitudes, complete flying control could be maintained at low flying speeds. Its 'N'-shaped interplane struts eliminated drag-producing rigging wires in the wings.

The D-VII first entered service on the Western Front in May 1918 during Germany's abortive spring offensive. Allied squadrons proved

The Fokker D VII was built at OAW Albatros Flugzeugwerke in 1918. This particular aircraft was given to the Swiss Air Force in 1926 for training purposes, but was returned to Germany in 1936, flown by the famous World War 1 fighter ace, Ernst Udet. The aircraft was destroyed by Allied bombs during World War 2 (Stapfer).

superior but throughout the summer and autumn the D-VII replaced inferior fighting scouts in the majority of Germany's *Jagdstaffeln*. Germany's fighter pilots soon took advantage of the D-VII's fast turn and other flying characteristics. A favourite form of attack was to hang the aircraft on its propeller below an Allied aircraft while firing the two synchronized Spandaus. *Rittmeister* Manfred Freiherr von Richtofen's famous 'Flying Circus' flew the Fokker D-VII in the Second Battle of Aisne in mid-1918. The D-VII was also the favourite mount of other German aces such as *Leutnant* Carl Degelow, CO of *Jagdstaffel* 40 who scored over twenty of his thirty confirmed victories flying a D-VII over a five-month period. Another was *Hauptmann* Rudolf Berthold, CO of *Jagdgeschwader Nr 2*, who finished the war with 44 confirmed victories.

By November 1918 almost 800 D-VIIs were in service with the German Army Air service but the type had arrived too late to influence the outcome of the air battle on the Western Front. It had proved such an outstanding adversary that the D-VII was specially referred to under the reperation clauses at the Treaty of Versailles. However, some examples managed to reach Holland where Fokker continued producing this outstanding fighter in limited numbers.

GENERAL DYNAMICS F-16A FIGHTING FALCON

Type Air combat fighter. **Crew** (F-16A/C) Pilot only. (F-16B/D) Dual seat. **Manufacturers** General Dynamics, Fort Worth, Texas. Sub-contracted by Sonaca/SABA, Belgium and Fokker-VFW, Holland. **Power plant** One 25,000 lb reheat Pratt & Whitney F100-PW-200 turbofan or one 27,000 lb General Electric F110-GE-100 augmented turbofan. **Dimensions** Span, 31 ft. Length, 47 ft 7¾ in. Height, 16 ft 5¼ in **Weight** Empty, 14,567 lb. Loaded, 22,785 lb. **Performance** Max speed, 1,255 mph at 36,000 ft. 915 mph at sea level. Service ceiling, 52,000 ft. **Armament** One 20 mm M61A-1 Vulcan rotary cannon. Two-to-six AIM-9 Sidewinder missiles and maximum external ordnance load of 15,200 lb with reduced internal fuel or 11,000 lb with full internal fuel.

The F-16A derives from the USAF Lightweight Fighter Prototype programme which was an exercise established to evaluate and examine developments in advanced aircraft technology and design. From among five original contenders in April 1972 the USAF finally selected two competitors, the General Dynamics YF-16 and the Northrop YF-17. The first YF-16 prototype was rolled out in December 1973 and the aircraft flew for the first time in February 1974.

By mid-1974 the LWF programme became more than an exercise in technology with the conclusion that the winner could receive substantial export orders from four NATO countries wishing to replace their ageing F-104G Starfighters. In late 1974 the Lightweight Fighter was being called the Air Combat Fighter (ACF).

In January 1975 the USAF selected the YF-16 as its Air Combat Fighter in preference to the YF-17, primarily because of its lower production and operating costs, better range, lower aerodynamic drag, better manouevrability above Mach .8 and overall weight factor. The F-16A is only half the weight of the F-4 Phantom and has a number of advanced technologies, notably fly-by-wire flight controls actuated by a side stick force controller, high 'G' tolerance, 30° reclined seat and single piece bubble canopy, automatic variable wing leading-edge flaps and decreased weight as a result of composite materials used in its construction.

Also in January 1975 the USAF announced plans calling for at least 650 aircraft. On 7 June the European consortium of Belgium, Denmark, Norway and The Netherlands announced that they planned to purchase 348 F-16s. In July 1976 the first European co-production contract was signed. Final airframe assembly lines for the

Two advanced F–16Cs (foreground) and two F–16As (rear) of 312 Tactical Fighter training squadron at Luke Air Force Base, Arizona (General Dynamics).

European aircraft were established in 1978 in Belgium and The Netherlands. Belgium also provides final assembly of the F100 engine for the European aircraft.

The first of eight pre-production aircraft flew for the first time on 8 December 1976 and the first full production aircraft made its inaugural flight on 7 August 1978. The F-16A first entered service with the 388th TFW at Hill AFB, Utah on 6 January 1979. The F-16C has improved radar, avionics and increased structural strength for greater weapons load. Its initial flight was made on 19 June 1984 and deliveries to the USAF began in July that year.

F-16s currently equip ten fighter wings and units in the US Air Reserve Forces. Altogether, 3,047 Falcons are on order for the USAF. In NATO the F-16A equips the air forces of Belgium (which has ordered 160 aircraft), The Netherlands (213), Denmark (70), Norway (72), Greece (60) and Turkey (160). In addition, eight other countries have ordered the F-16 taking total production orders to 4,346 aircraft.

In 1985 General Dynamics proposed a specially configured Falcon, the F-16SC, to meet specific USAF defence requirements at a cost below that of the F-16C. Several companies are competing for this programme, which calls for an interceptor force of 300 aircraft.

Above *The Bristol F 2B Fighter preserved by the Shuttleworth Trust at Old Warden airfield, Bedfordshire* (Author).

Below *Lightning T Mk 5 of the LTF, RAF Binbrook, pictured taking off from RAF Upper Heyford on 18 July 1981* (Author).

Above *F-16A Fighting Falcon of the 50th TFW, Hahn, Germany photographed in June 1983 (Author).*

Right *Hawker Hunter F GA 6 of 229 OCU RAF Chivenor, April 1974 (MOD).*

Below *Buccaneer S2As of 208 Squadron Strike Command near Beachy Head in July 1985 (MOD).*

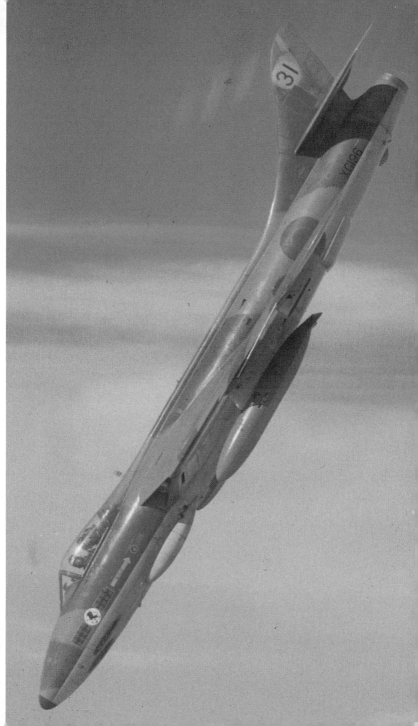

Above *F–104G Starfighter of the* Luftwaffe *in May 1985* (Author).

Below *Phantom FGR2 of 'Treble One' Squadron, Leuchars photographed in May 1985* (Author).

A television-guided Maverick missile is fired from an F-16B fighter in a demonstration sortie over California. Typically the aircraft is loaded with six Mavericks, two 370-gallon external fuel tanks, and two Sidewinder air-to-air missiles.

GLOSTER GLADIATOR

Type Fighter. Sea Gladiator: carrier-borne fighter. **Crew** Pilot only. **Manufacturers** Gloster Aircraft Company. **Power plant** One 840 hp Bristol Mercury IX. **Dimensions** Span, 32 ft 3 in. Length, 27 ft 5 in. Height, 10 ft 4 in. **Weight** Empty, 3,450 lb. Loaded, 4,750 lb. **Performance** Max speed, 253 mph. Service ceiling, 33,000 ft. Range 440 miles. **Armament** (late models) Two .303 in Browning machine-guns in fuselage, one .303 Browning under each wing.

This remarkable, sturdy biplane fighter served with the RAF and twelve other air forces. It fought on the side of the Chinese in the defence of Canton during the Sino-Japanese war, took part in the Arab Airpin operations in Palestine in 1938 and fought for the Finns against Russia in the so-called Winter War of November 1939 — March 1940. If the Munich crisis of 1938 had brought war with Germany, Britain would have been defended almost entirely by Gladiators and Gauntlets. Even in 1939, for every twelve Hurricanes and seven Spitfires, the RAF still had five Gladiators in its inventory.

The Gladiator was descended from a prototype first conceived in 1927. H. P. Holland's SS37 prototype first flew in September 1934 and conformed to Specification F7/30 which had produced an original three contenders, including the gull-winged Spitfire. Though a late entrant, the fabric-covered biplane was accepted and an order placed in July 1935 for 23 aircraft. By the time production had ceased in April 1940, 480 had been delivered to the RAF, 60 Sea Gladiators to the FAA and 216 to twelve other countries.

The Gladiator first entered RAF service with 72 Squadron in February 1937 and with 3 Squadron in March. At the outbreak of war Gladiators of 607 and 615 Squadrons of the AASF were sent to France. In May 1940 they fought against the *Luftwaffe* in Belgium and France and later defended the fleet at Scapa Flow. On 22 April 1940 263 Squadron flew its Gladiators aboard HMS *Glorious* at Scapa Flow and sailed to Norway to take part in the ill-fated campaign there. Royal Norwegian Air Force Gladiators had already been decimated by the *Luftwaffe* during the defence of Oslo but the RAF pilots found conditions much worse. All suitable airfields in Norway were in German control so on the evening of 24 April eighteen Gladiators of 263 Squadron landed on the frozen surface of Lake Lesjaskog, about forty miles from Aandalsnes. Despite maintenance and fuel problems 263 Squadron operated against appalling odds until 27 April when the last fuel supplies were exhausted. After setting fire to their surviving

Gloster Gladiator II fitted with skis for service with the Royal Norwegian Air Force.

Gladiators the pilots and crews were brought home on the cargo vessel *Delius* after running the gauntlet of dive-bombing attacks off the Norwegian coast.

On 14 May 263 Squadron, now equipped with eighteen Gladiator IIs, returned to Norway in HMS *Glorious* together with 804 Squadron's (FAA) Sea Gladiators. On 21 May two sections of Gladiators got into difficulties in a blinding snowstorm while attempting to reach Bardfoss near Narvik. A Swordfish and two Gladiators were lost when the force turned back although the other Flight miraculously found the *Glorious* and somehow put down on the heaving deck.

By 24 May fourteen Gladiators had managed to reach Bardfoss and for two weeks they fought a desperate battle against superior enemy aircraft. The Gladiators destroyed no fewer than 36 enemy aircraft for the loss of only two in combat. No 263 Squadron flew its last patrol on 7 June before being evacuated in *Glorious*. Tragically, on 8 June the aircraft carrier was sunk by concentrated fire from the battlecruisers *Scharnhorst* and *Gneisenau* and all ten pilots were lost.

From 11–28 June 1940 six Gladiators flown by RAF pilots (with another six in store) constituted the entire air defence of Malta. The first Italian air raid on the island took place on the morning of 11 June and the unescorted force of bombers was broken up by two of the Gladiators. However, contrary to the legend of '*Faith*, *Hope* and *Charity*,' only three air raids took place between 11–30 June and it is almost certain the 'six' Gladiators were so named for morale boosting purposes.

In August 1940 Gladiators equipped 247 Squadron at Roborough and were responsible for the defence of Plymouth Docks during the Battle of Britain.

The Gladiator's greatest successes were against the Regia Aeronautica in Greece prior to the Luftwaffe's involvement. By the end of 1940 Flight Lieutenant M. T. St. J. Pattle DFC is known to have shot down at least 24 enemy aircraft in a Gladiator while flying from bases in Greece. (Pattle, a South-African, later converted to Hurricanes and had scored 41 confirmed kills before he was killed in 1941). On 28 February 1941 28 Gladiators and Hurricanes attacked about fifty Italian aircraft over the Greco-Albanian border and destroyed 27 in ninety minutes and a further eleven probables. The only other casualty was one Gladiator which force-landed. The Sea Gladiator was largely superseded as a first-line fighter by the Grumman Martlet by the end of 1940. Although the Gladiator continued its first-line service with the RAF until only 1941 it was also used in other roles, notably on meteorological flights, until 1945.

GLOSTER METEOR I-IV

Type Fighter. **Crew** Pilot only. **Manufacturers** Gloster Aircraft Company. (Some F4s) Sub-contracted by Armstrong Whitworth. **Power plant** (F1) Two Rolls-Royce Welland centrifugal turbojets (F4) Two Rolls-Royce Derwent 5s. **Dimensions** (F1) Span, 43 ft. Length, 41 ft 4 ins. Height, 13 ft. **Weight** (F1), Empty, 8,140 lb. Loaded, 13,800 lb. **Performance** Max speed, (Mk I) 410 mph at 30,000 ft. Service ceiling, 40,000 ft. (F4) 550 mph at 30,000 ft. Service ceiling, 50,000 ft. **Armament** (F1 & F4) Four 20 mm Hispano cannon.

Towards the end of the Second World War German jet fighters such as the Me 262 and rocket fighters like the Me 263 were seen regularly by Allied bomber crews. Britain was not far behind in jet fighter design and by 1945 had gained a world lead which was not seriously challenged by America until 1947.

The Gloster G41 was designed to specification F9/40, drawn up in August 1940 after consultation with George Carter of Glosters by the Air Ministry. It was finally issued in December 1940, just five months before the maiden flight of the Gloster G40 (E28/39) experimental single-jet prototype whose power plant was designed by Frank (later Sir Frank) Whittle. Carter decided upon a twin-engined layout because of the relatively low thrust available in the early type of turbojet engine. On 7 February 1941 twelve F9/40 prototypes were ordered from Glosters and it was intended that various types of engines would be used in these prototypes. Several British companies were engaged in jet engine research, including the pioneer firm of Pioneer Jets Ltd. Rover and Metrovick were building the prototype power plants.

The first Meteor to be completed was fitted with Rover-built W2B turbojets but the engines failed to produce more than 1,000 lb of thrust each and made only taxi-ing trials. At the controls was P. E. G. Sayer, who on 15 May 1941 had made the first flight by a British powered jet-propelled aircraft when he piloted the E28/39 at Cranwell. It was not until 5 March 1943 that the fifth prototype, powered by Halford HI turbojets (forerunner of the de Havilland Goblin), each of which developed 1,500 lb thrust, became the first Meteor to achieve sustained flight. Work on the remaining prototypes continued throughout 1943, their number having been reduced to eight. The powerplant finally chosen was the Rolls-Royce W2B/23 Welland of 1,700 lb thrust. The fourth prototype using these engines was first flown on 12 June 1943 at Barford St John.

By the end of 1943 five prototype Meteors had flown, two of which

F4 Meteors of No 222 Squadron, RAF Leuchars crossing the Firth of Forth. These were the first jets ever stationed in Scotland (Jerry Cullum).

had been powered by the Welland. The first production Meteor Mk I was sent to the USA in February 1944 in exchange for a Bell YP-59 Airacomet as part of an Anglo-American agreement reached in mid-1943. An order was placed by the Air Ministry for twenty Meteor Mk Is and the type began equipping 616 Squadron at Culmhead on 12 July 1944. At the end of the month this unit began moving to Manston, Kent for operations against V1 flying bombs being directed at London. Altogether, seven Meteors and two Flights of Spitfire IXs made the trip (the squadron finally converted entirely to Meteors in August 1944).

The first V1 sortie by a Meteor was made on 27 July 1944 but for a whole week gun stoppages prevented the pilots from dealing effectively with the 'Doodlebugs'. Flying Officer Dean was on patrol on 4 August when his guns failed to fire but he succeeded in tipping over a V1 with his own wing-tip. It crashed out of control near Tonbridge without causing any damage. Within a few days three more V1s had been brought down, this time using guns (two of them by Dean). With the Allied occupation of the *pas de Calais* and its major V1 sites, Meteor pilots found increasingly rare pickings. However, just eight days after the Meteor entered service with the RAF, nine Me 262s of KG51 became operational with the Luftwaffe. The East Anglian-based American 8th Air Force had most to fear from the new jets which could have caused havoc with the mass formations of Liberators and Fortresses had they been available in quantity. In October 1944 Meteors were used in mock attacks to help enable American gunners and fighter pilots devise the most effective defence tactics for use against the German jets. The exercise also provided the Meteor pilots with useful experience for the anticipated jet fighter combat on the continent.

Early in 1945 a Flight of Meteor IIIs, the first of which had flown in September 1944, was detached to join the Second Tactical Air Force in Europe. At first operational sorties on the continent were restricted to flights over friendly territory to avoid any of the new aircraft falling into enemy hands. Later, when the remainder of 616 Squadron joined the flight at Nijmegen, the Luftwaffe had almost been swept from the skies and the restrictions were lifted. A number of Meteor raids were made on the German homeland but no combat with Me 262s was ever reported.

A second Meteor Squadron, No 504, arrived in Europe before the cessation of hostilities. The first fifteen Meteor IIIs were fitted with Welland engines but subsequent batches were fitted with the new 2,000 lb thrust Derwent 1, which became standard equipment on all later Meteors. It also differed from the Mk 1 in having increased fuel tankage and a backwards-sliding hood in place of the sideways-opening hood fitted to early Meteors. Altogether, over 200 Meteor IIIs were built.

Post-war the Meteor F3 served with the RAF and Auxiliary squadrons and was replaced in first-line service by the Meteor F4 in 1948. The Meteor F4 differed in having uprated Derwent 5 engines. On 7 November 1945 Group Captain H. J. Wilson of the RAF High-Speed Flight established a new World Air Speed Record of 606 mph flying a Meteor F4. On 7 September 1946 Group Captain E. M. Donaldson increased the record to 616 mph in a Meteor F4.

Altogether, 465 Meteor F4s were built for the RAF, including 40 by Armstrong Whitworth. From 1950 the Meteor F4 began to be replaced in RAF service by the F8. The 'Meatbox' will always be remembered as the only Allied jet aircraft to see operational service in World War Two.

GRUMMAN F4F WILDCAT

Type Carrier-borne or shore-based fighter. **Crew** Pilot only. **Manufacturers** Grumman Aircraft Engineering Corp, Bethpage, Long Island, New York. Sub-contracted by the Eastern Division, General Motors. **Power plant** (Mk I) One Wright Cyclone G-205A (Mk II) One Pratt & Whitney Twin Wasp S3C4-G. **Dimensions** Span, 38 ft. Length, 28 ft 10 in. Height, 9 ft 2½ in. **Weight** Empty, 4,649 lb. Loaded, 6,100 lb. **Performance** Max speed, (Mk I) 310 mph, (IV) 330 mph at 19,500 ft. Max range, (IV) 1,150 miles. Service ceiling, 28,000 ft. **Armament** (Mk I) Four .50 calibre machine-guns in wings. (II & IV), six .50 calibre machine-guns in wings.

One of the most outstanding fleet fighters of the Second World War and the US Navy's standard carrier-borne fighter from 1941 to 1943. The XF4F-1 was designed in 1935 as a biplane to continue Grumman's long line of F3F series fighters for the US Navy. In 1936 the concept was changed to a mid-wing monoplane single-seat fighter and eventually emerged as the XF4F-3 in 1939. France ordered 91 fixed-wing F4F-3s but following the German invasion in 1940 all were diverted to Britain and named Martlet I. In 1941 the US Navy, which had placed an order for 78 F4F-3s in 1940, adopted the name Wildcat. The type continued to be known as the Martlet in British service until January 1944 when Britain reverted to the American name as part of inter-Allied standardization in designations.

The first six Martlets arrived in the UK in August 1940 and the type first entered service with 804 Squadron at Hatson on 8 September. On Christmas Day 1940 the Martlet became the first type of American fighter in service with British forces to shoot down a German aircraft.

A Wildcat taxi-ing into position after landing on HMS Biter *(Cooper).*

Grumman F4F-4 of the US Navy in flight with freshly painted national insignia (Grumman).

Lieutenant L. V. Carver and Sub Lieutenant Parke achieved this feat when they forced down a Junkers Ju 88 attempting to bomb the British Home Fleet at Scapa Flow.

The Martlet II, introduced in March 1941, differed from the Mk I in having folding wings and a Pratt & Whitney Twin Wasp engine in place of the earlier Wright Cyclone. The Mk II was ideally suited for small escort carrier operations and gave sterling service during the Malta convoys and during operations over Madagascar in May 1942.

Although slower than other American fighters and out-performed by the Japanese Zero, in the Pacific theatre the Wildcat averaged almost seven enemy aircraft shot down to every one F4F lost. This can be attributed to its rugged construction and the skill of its pilots. One of the most memorable feats attributed to this aircraft occurred on 20 February 1942. US Navy Lieutenant Commander Edward 'Butch' O'Hare single-handedly saved his carrier, *Lexington*, by breaking up an attack of nine Japanese bombers and shooting down five of them in six minutes. O'Hare became one of the first American aces and was awarded the Medal of Honour.

Altogether, some 8,000 Wildcats were built from 1939 to 1942.

GRUMMAN F6F HELLCAT

Type Carrier-borne day/night fighter. **Crew** Pilot only. **Manufacturers** Grumman Aircraft Engineering Corporation, Bethpage, Long Island, New York. **Specification (Hellcat II) — Power plant** One 2,000 hp Pratt & Whitney Double Wasp R-2800-10W. **Dimensions** Span, 42 ft 10 in. Length, 33 ft 7 in. Height, 14 ft 5 in. **Weight** Empty, 9,212 lb. Loaded, 13,753 lb maximum. **Performance** Max speed, 371 mph at 17,200 ft. Range, 1,040 miles at 159 mph. Service ceiling 36,700 ft. **Armament** Six .50 calibre machine-guns in wings. Provision for six 60 lb rocket-projectiles under outer wing panels or two 1,000 lb bombs under centre fuselage section.

Like so many Grumman fighters the Hellcat's claim to fame lies in the Pacific. It was designed as a replacement for the Grumman Wildcat in US Navy service and first took to the air at Bethpage, Long Island on 26 June 1942. The F6F first entered combat with VF-5 US Navy Squadron of USS *Yorktown* and VF-9 of USS *Essex* on 31 August 1943 with strikes against Marcus Island. From thenceforth the Hellcat

In RAF colours, Grumman Hellcat 1, FN376 (Charles E. Brown).

showed a marked superiority against Japanese aircraft, serving with the majority of US Navy and Marine Corps squadrons in the Pacific theatre.

By the close of 1943 approximately 2,500 Hellcats had been delivered to operational squadrons. Almost 75 per cent of all the US Navy's air-to-air victories were attributed to the F6F, with a ratio of 19:1, destroying 4,947 enemy aircraft plus another 209 claimed by land-based units. The pinnacle of its glittering Pacific career was reached during the Battle of the Philippine Sea (19-20 June 1944) when the Hellcat effectively halted the Japanese attack on the first day, accounting for most of the 300 aircraft lost by the Japanese Air Force.

Originally, the Hellcat I supplied to Britain was known as the Gannet I and was the British equivalent of the US Navy F6F-3. The Hellcat began equipping 800 Squadron in July 1943. Altogether, 252 Hellcat Is were issued to the FAA and were followed by the Hellcat II which differed from the Mk 1 in having an up-rated engine. Some 74 of the 930 Hellcat IIs were fitted with an underwing radome and painted midnight-blue for night fighter operations. Hellcats first equipped 800 Squadron in July 1943 which embarked in the light escort-carrier

A US Navy Grumman F6F Hellcat. The plane's claim to fame rests on its performance in the Pacific Theatre during World War 2 (Grumman).

Emperor in December that year. The squadron's first actions included anti-shipping strikes off the coast of Norway and in April 1944 Hellcats took part in the attack on the *Tirpitz* in Kaafiord. Hellcats of 1840 Squadron later escorted another strike on the German battleship in August 1944.

By the end of 1944 some six squadrons of FAA Hellcats were in service with the British Pacific Fleet, seeing action off Malaya. In January 1945 16 Hellcats of 1839 and 1844 Squadrons from HMS *Indomitable* took part in the large-scale raids on Japanese oil refineries at Pangkalan Brandan and Palembang. On 2 May 1945 800 Squadron Hellcats provided fighter-cover during the capture of Rangoon. In mid-1945 twelve squadrons were equipped with the Hellcat but by August 1946 the type had been phased out of FAA service, most having been returned to the USA under the terms of Lend-Lease.

By the time production ceased in November 1945, some 12,275 Hellcats had been produced. In addition to service with the US Navy and the FAA, the F6F also saw service with the French Air Force and Navy and the Argentine and Uruguayan navies. Beginning on 28 August 1952 modified F6F-5K pilotless drones, each carrying a 2,000 lb bomb, were launched from the USS *Boxer* against North Korean targets.

GRUMMAN F-14 TOMCAT

Type Air superiority fighter. **Crew** Two. **Manufacturers** Grumman Aerospace. **Power plant** Two Pratt & Whitney TF30-P-412A turbofans. **Dimensions** Span, 64 ft 1½ in. Length, 61 ft 11⅞ in. Height, 16 ft. **Weight** Empty, 40,070 lb. Loaded, 68,567 lb. **Performance** Max speed, (clean) 1,545 mph at 40,000 ft. Service ceiling, 60,000 ft. **Armament** One 20 mm Vulcan M-61A1 rotary cannon and six AIM-7E/F Sparrow and four AIM-9G/H Sidewinder or six AIM-54A and two AIM-9G/H air-to-air-missiles. (It is also capable of carrying the Phoenix long-range missile.)

In February 1969 Grumman signed the contract to build the replacement for the Navy's aging F-4 Phantom. The Tomcat is now one of the world's most formidable long-range strike aircraft and is also excellent for close-in dog-fighting. The Hughes Aircraft AWG-9 Weapons Control System radar gives the backseat Weapons Control Officer the ability to track 24 enemy targets and simultaneously attack six different threats at varied altitudes and distances.

The Tomcat's conception took root during the early 1960s when the US Navy saw a requirement for a high-performance fighter that could operate from aircraft carriers in all weathers and fly long distances at high speed to intercept and destroy any enemy aircraft or missile before they posed a threat to the fleet.

Any of combination of Phoenix, Sidewinder or Sparrow missiles may be fitted to compliment the F-14's internal M161 cannon. This Tomcat of the F-32 sports Phoenix missiles; its advanced weapons guidance system allows it to fire simultaneously at different targets up to 100 miles away (Grumman).

With wings swept forward, three US Navy Grumman F-14A Tomcats parade in close formation.

Titanium metal and composite materials were used in the Tomcat's construction for decreased structural weight and the horizontal stabilizer skins were the first composite production components built for any aircraft. The automatically-positioned wings sweep to 68° for high-speed manoeuvring but when fully extended permit take-offs in less than 1,000 feet and landings in less than 2,000 feet at speeds below 120 knots. Positioned by computer, the wing angle is dependent on the speed of the aircraft.

After a two-year design and development period the first of twelve research and development aircraft made its maiden flight on 21 December 1970. The first production aircraft was delivered to the US Navy in June 1972 and for two years the US Navy carried out its

evaluation of the type. When the Tomcat began deployment with the US Navy, with VF-1 and VF-2, initially on the aircraft carrier USS *Enterprise* in September 1974, it was the world's first operational air superiority fighter with a variable-sweep wing. Since then, some 26 F-14 squadrons have been deployed world-wide.

The F-14C introduced new avionics and weapons systems and the F-14D is scheduled to begin development flight testing in the summer of 1986. This version will have F110-GE-400 engines of 56,000 lb thrust, a vastly improved radar and advanced digital avionics. In addition, it will carry new defensive ECM equipment, the JTIDS (Joint Tactical Information Distribution System) and an IRST (Infra-Red Search and Track set).

A total of 601 Tomcats were ordered by the US Navy (including the twelve prototypes). Some 79 Tomcats were delivered to the Imperial Iranian Air Force and by 23 April 1986 533 F-14s had been built for the US Navy.

HAWKER DEMON

Type Fighter. **Crew** Two. **Manufacturers** Hawker Aircraft Ltd, Kingston, Surrey. Sub-contracted by Boulton Paul. **Power plant** One 485 hp Rolls-Royce Kestrel IIS or 584 hp V (DR). **Dimensions** Span, 37 ft 3 in. Length, 29 ft 7 in. Height, 10 ft 5 in. **Weight** Empty, 3,067 lb. Loaded, 4,464 lb. **Performance** (Kestrel V) Max speed, 182 mph at 16,400 ft. Service ceiling, 27,500 ft. **Armament** Twin Vickers guns forward and one Lewis gun aft. Small bombs below wings.

The Demon was a two-seat fighter derivative of the Hart bomber and was the first of its type since the First World War. The prototype was a converted Hart bomber fitted with a fully supercharged Rolls-Royce Kestrel IIS, twin front guns and a cut-away rear cockpit with a tilted gun ring for improved field of fire. Originally, the production models

The Hawker Demon was a three-gun development of the Hawker Hart bomber. 23 Squadron aircraft here line up for the camera (Flight).

were called Hart fighters until the name Demon was conferred upon it in July 1932.

The first of a pre-production batch of six Hart fighters made its maiden flight on 22 June 1931 and the first production Demon flew for the first time in February 1933. By April 1933 23 Squadron, which had received one Flight of Demons in March 1931, had converted entirely to Demons from Bulldogs. A total of 128 Demons was built by Hawkers before production was transferred to Boulton Paul in 1935. From October 1936 all Boulton Paul-built Demons were fitted with a Fraser-Nash hydraulically-operated turret with a 'lobster back' shield to protect the rear gunner from the effects of slipstream. These aircraft were subsequently known as Turret Demons and many other earlier models were retrofitted with the device. Boulton Paul built 106 Demons, bringing the number delivered to the RAF by December 1937 to 234 in all. Demons served with eleven fighter squadrons in the UK and four overseas until replaced in front-line service by the Blenheim I in 1939.

HAWKER FURY I/II

Type Interceptor fighter. **Crew** Pilot only. **Manufacturers** Hawker Aircraft Ltd, Kingston, Surrey. Sub-Power contracted by General Aircraft. **Specification (Fury II) — Power plant** One 640 hp Rolls-Royce Kestrel VI. **Dimensions** Span, 30 ft. Length, 26 ft 9 in. Height, 10 ft 2 in. **Weight** Empty, 2,743 lb. Loaded, 3,609 lb. **Performance** Max speed, 223 mph at 16,400 ft. Service ceiling, 29,500 ft. **Armament** Twin, synchronized Vickers machine-guns.

The Fury I was developed from two earlier Hawker fighters, the Mercury-engined F20/27 of 1928 and the Hornet of 1929. It was accepted by the Air Staff after competitive trials with the Fairey Firefly IIM and became the RAF's standard interceptor. It was also the first RAF fighter in squadron service to exceed 200 mph, faster than the standard day/night fighters of the day. The Fury also possessed an amazing rate of climb of 2,380 ft/min.

The Fury I began equipping 43 Squadron at Tangmere, Sussex in May-June 1931 and eventually equipped a further two RAF squadrons. When production ceased in 1935, 117 had been built for the RAF. It was followed on the Hawker production lines by the Fury II which was built as an interim replacement before the introduction of the monoplane Hurricane. The Fury II's design was based on the intermediate and high speed Furies and marked a significant increase in performance over the Fury I, being 8 per cent faster and boasting a 34 per cent increase in rate of climb. The prototype Fury II made its maiden flight in December 1936 and production models began equipping 25 Squadron at Hawkinge early the following year. A further four squadrons equipped with the Fury II but all had been replaced by Gladiators, Hurricanes and Spitfires by 1939. A total of 108 Fury IIs was built for the RAF and South African Air Force.

Right *In late 1936, 25 Squadron became the first in the RAF to receive the Hawker Fury II, an event commemorated by this neatly stacked formation* (Aeroplane).

HAWKER HURRICANE I

Type Fighter. **Crew** Pilot only. **Manufacturers** Hawker Aircraft Ltd, Kingston, Surrey. Sub-contracted by Gloster Aircraft Co. **Power plant** One 1,030 hp Rolls-Royce Merlin II or III. **Dimensions** Span, 40 ft. Length, 31 ft 5 in. Height, 13 ft 1½ in. **Weight** Empty, 4,670 lb. Loaded, 6,600 lb. **Performance** Max speed, 318 mph at 17,500 ft. Service ceiling, 33,200 ft. **Armament** Eight .303 in Browning machine-guns.

The most famous in the long line of Hawker single-seat fighters which, together with the Spitfire, was responsible for the defeat of the *Luftwaffe* in the Battle of Britain and later served on no fewer than seventeen different fronts. Sydney (later Sir Sydney) Camm's immortal design took shape in 1930 when the Air Staff issued Specification F7/30 for a monoplane fighter with four machine-guns and based on the Rolls-Royce steam cooled in-line Goshawk engine. At that time Camm was committed to the development of variants of the Hart and Fury biplane types for the RAF and foreign air forces but he responded with a monoplane design based on the Fury I but with a spatted, fixed undercarriage and four guns; two in the fuselage and two in the wings.

Camm's design, like that of Mitchell's at Vickers Supermarine (Mitchell was also working to the F7/30 Specification), was altered on the drawing board with the decision in January 1934 to proceed with the new Rolls-Royce PV12 engine (later more famous as the Merlin). Simultaneously, the 'Fury Monoplane' was re-named the 'Interceptor Monoplane'.

Negotiations were in progress in 1934 to adapt the American Colt .300 Browning machine-gun to fire .303 rimless calibre ammunition and manufacture the gun under licence in Britain. The Colt-Browning was noted for its compactness and operating reliability. In July 1935 an agreement was finally reached between Colt and the Birmingham Small Arms Company so the Air Ministry specification was amended to incorporate eight .303 inch Browning machine-guns in the Hawker Monoplane.

Camm's team had other problems to contend with. Requirements such as retractable undercarriage, wing-flaps, wheel brakes, blind flying instrumentation and radio, were all relatively unexplored territories in 1935.

Construction techniques were also different from what had gone before. Although the Hurricane was fabric covered, its construction was tubular steel. However, the Hurricane proved easier to build than the Spitfire which used a metal stressed-skin monocoque structure

Hurricane Is of III Squadron; by September 1939 Hurricane Is equipped eighteen squadrons of the RAF.

with only the control surfaces being fabric-covered. As a result the Hawker design was completed in prototype form in nine months at Kingston-Upon-Thames. It was moved by road to the Hawker airfield at Brooklands for its maiden flight on 6 November 1935. Flight Lieutenant P. W. S. Bulman, the company's chief test pilot, reported remarkable manoeuvrability and docility, characteristics confirmed through later initial trials. The Hurricane's relatively uncomplicated construction (when compared to the Spitfire), permitted quantity production to begin at once.

In June 1936 'Scheme F' was issued calling for the production of 500 Hurricanes and 300 Spitfires within three years. An order for a further 400 Hurricanes was issued in November 1938 and as a result production had to be sub-contracted to the Gloster Company. By September 1939 497 Hurricanes had been built and by 7 August 1940 2,309 Hurricanes had been delivered (against 1,383 Spitfires).

The first production Hurricane had made its maiden flight on 12 October 1937 and differed from the prototype in having a 1,030 hp Rolls-Royce Merlin II engine, modified cockpit canopy and exhaust pipes and a re-designed undercarriage fairing. The first Hurricanes to come off the production lines were fitted with two-bladed, fixed-pitch wooden propellers; later models were fitted with de Havilland or Rotol constant-speed airscrews. In 1939 metal-covered wings began to replace the fabric-covered wings on the production lines.

The Hurricane I first entered service with 111 Squadron at Northolt on 15 December 1937 where it replaced the Gauntlet. In January 1938 Hurricanes replaced Gloster Gladiators of No 3 Squadron at Kenley, Surrey. In February Squadron Leader J. E. Gillan, CO of 111 Squadron, flew a Hurricane I from Edinburgh to Northolt at an average speed of 408 mph assisted by a strong tail wind at 17,000 ft; a fact which acquired him the nickname 'Downwind' Gillan for all time!

By September 1939, Hurricane Is equipped eighteen squadrons of the RAF and by early August 1940 this had risen to 32 squadrons (the Spitfire equipped 18½ squadrons). Four Hurricane squadrons were despatched to France at the outbreak of war as part of the Advanced Air Striking Force and the Air Component. In the first twelve months of the war, up until the end of the Battle of Britain, the Hurricane shot down more than 1,500 enemy aircraft.

For his actions on 17 August 1940 Flight Lieutenant J. B. Nicholson of 249 Squadron was awarded the first and only Fighter Command Victoria Cross for shooting down an Me 110 over Southampton after he had been badly wounded and his Hurricane set on fire. Other famous fighter pilots whose first victories began to accumulate in Hurricanes during the Battle of Britain included; Flight Lieutenant Robert Stanford Tuck of 257 Squadron (10 confirmed + 1 shared); Flight Lieutenant Douglas Bader of 242 Squadron; Sergeant Pilot J. H. 'Ginger' Lacey (15 + 1 shared); and Sergeant Pilot J. Frantisek of 303 Squadron (17) — the top scoring Czech and Allied pilot. Frantisek scored all seventeen victories during September 1940 and was killed on 9 October the same year. In the Battle of Britain the Hurricane was flown by about six in every ten squadrons and it accounted for more enemy aircraft destroyed than any other type of British aircraft.

HAWKER TYPHOON

Type Close-support fighter and fighter-bomber. **Crew** Pilot only. **Manufacturers** Hawker Aircraft Co Ltd, Langley, Bucks. (15 aircraft only). Gloster Aircraft Co Ltd, Hucclecote, Gloucester. **Specification (Typhoon IB) — Power plant** One 2,180 hp Napier Sabre IIA, 2,200 hp Sabre IIB or 2,260 hp Sabre IIC. **Dimensions** Span, 41 ft 7 in. Length, 31 ft 11 in. Height, 15 ft 3½ in. **Weight** Empty, 8,800 lb. Loaded, 13,250 lb. **Performance** Max speed, 412 mph at 19,000 ft. Range, 510 miles with bombs or 980 miles with no bombs and auxiliary fuel tanks. Service ceiling, 35,200 ft. **Armament** Four 20 mm cannon in wings and provision for two 1,000 lb bombs or eight 60 lb rocket-projectiles below the wings.

The Typhoon was conceived by Sydney Camm in 1937 as a future Hurricane replacement and developed in parallel with the Vulture-engined Tornado to Specification F18/37. The Air Ministry decided to ignore conventional engines such as the Centaurus and Griffon and concentrate instead on the complex and untried Vulture and Sabre power plants. The former powered the 'R' type fighter (later named Tornado) and the latter the 'N' type fighter (later named Typhoon). The Tornado programme was eventually abandoned early in 1941 but the Typhoon-Sabre programme went ahead. As it turned out, the Typhoon proved to be a disappointment in its designed role as an interceptor fighter. Despite producing a top speed of some 400 mph the Sabre proved unreliable, giving a disappointing performance at high altitudes and a poor rate of climb.

The Typhoon first entered service in September 1941 and the Sabre continued its teething problems for a good year after that. Problems too were encountered with the stub exhausts whose carbon monoxide fumes entered the cockpit, sometimes in sufficient quantity to nauseate pilots. More seriously, the tail assembly had a nasty tendency to come apart, causing many accidents. At one time it was even considered withdrawing the Typhoon from service but by the end of 1942 the 'Tiffies' structural problems had been cured and a progressive solution found for the Sabre's teething troubles.

The Typhoon Mk 1B, which differed from the IA in having four 20 mm cannon in place of the earlier twelve machine-guns, was the first type to see action, during the ill-fated Dieppe operation of 19 August 1942. From May 1942 the Typhoon demonstrated just how effective it could be on low-level operations when it was employed in defeating the Fw 190, which was making 'hit and run' raids along the south coast of England. Soon the Typhoon began to gain a reputation for 'hit and run' raids of its own. It was used repeatedly for 'train busting'

Background photograph *The aggressive lines of the Typhoon and the wing-mounted 20 mm cannons are evident in this view of Typhoon IA, R7646. Note the 'Austin 7' doors* (British Aerospace).

Inset *In service with No 183 Squadron, Typhoon IB, JP128* (British Aerospace).

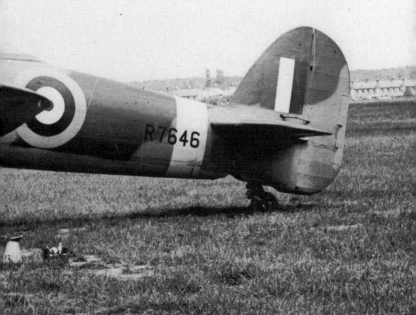

operations on the continent carrying two 250 lb bombs beneath its wings. By mid-1943 as many as 150 locomotives were being destroyed each month.

The Typhoon was later modified to carry rocket projectiles and played a vital part in the events leading up to D-Day, destroying German radar stations along the Channel coast. By 6 June 1944 the Typhoon formed the backbone of the 2nd Tactical Air Force, equipping some 26 squadrons. Their effectiveness was increased by what became known as the 'Cab Rank' system, whereby formations of Typhoons maintained standing patrols over the battle front ready for immediate action in support of the ground forces. The Typhoon achieved its most outstanding success during the ground battles at Caen and Falaise shortly after D-Day, when they wrought havoc behind enemy lines. During a single day Typhoons knocked out 175 tanks and vehicles in the Falaise gap. On 17 July 1944 Wing Commander Johnny Baldwin led 193 Squadron in the now famous attack on a convoy of German staff cars retreating from Caen in northern France. One of their victims was Field Marshal Erwin Rommel, who was badly wounded in the attack.

By October 1944 Typhoon squadrons were operating close to the Dutch border and caused the retreating German armies even greater problems along their lines of communication. On 24 October five squadrons of Typhoons, led by Group Captain D. E. Gillam, raided the HQ of the German 15th Army at Dordrecht, Holland, completely destroying the target and killing over seventy German staff officers.

Typhoons continued to give ground support to the Allied armies until the crossing of the Rhine. After VE Day Typhoon squadrons were rapidly disbanded or re-equipped and by the end of 1945 none remained in first-line service. A total of 3,330 Typhoons was built, including 3,315 by Gloster.

HAWKER HUNTER

Type Fighter, fighter-bomber and fighter-reconaissance. **Crew** Pilot only.
Manufacturers Hawker Aircraft (now British Aerospace). Produced under licence in Belgium and Holland. **Power plant** One Rolls-Royce Avon turbojet.
Dimensions Span, 33 ft 8 in. Length, 45 ft 10½ in. Height, 13 ft 2 in. **Weight** Empty, 12,128 lb. Loaded, 16,200 lb. **Performance** Max speed, 710 mph at sea level. 620 mph at altitude. Service ceiling, 50,000 ft. Range 490 miles (with external tanks), 1,840 miles. **Armament** Four 30 mm Aden cannon in gun pack below cockpit with provision for two 1,000 lb bombs and 24 3 in rockets in underwing pylons.

British fighters had been among the world's finest during World War Two and despite post-war cuts in defence spending continued to produce advanced designs such as the superlative Hawker Hunter; surely the most classic jet fighter of all time. It is undoubtably Britain's most successful post-war jet fighter with sales to more than seventeen air forces.

The Hunter first flew in prototype form on 20 July 1951. Two months later it was making high speed passes in excess of 700 mph at the Farnborough Air Show. The second prototype flew on 5 May 1952 and introduced a gun pack containing four Aden cannon. The third flew for the first time on 30 November 1952 with a Sapphire engine in place of the 6,500 lb thrust Avon 100 and became the prototype Hunter F2.

The first production Hunter F1 made its maiden flight at Dunsfold, Surrey on 16 May 1953 but further progress was halted when the Air Ministry insisted that an air brake be fitted. The Hunter F1 finally entered service in late July 1954 when it began equipping 43 Squadron at Leuchars, Scotland. Two other Squadrons, 54 at Odiham and 222, also at Leuchars, were later equipped with the F1 but problems with engine surge when the guns were fired at certain altitudes led to the type mainly being issued to OCUs. This embarrassment was eliminated on the F2 by the installation of the 8,000 lb thrust Sapphire 101 and the type entered service with 257 and 263 Squadrons at Wattisham, Suffolk, at the end of 1954.

Some 139 F1s were built by Hawkers at Kingston and Blackpool and only 45 F2s were built by Armstrong Whitworth before production switched to the F4. The F3 designation had been applied to the original prototype Hunter in 1953 when it had been fitted with a re-heated Avon RA7R engine. That year it captured the World Speed Record at 727.6 mph. The F4 differed from the F1 and F2 mainly in having additional fuel capacity and provision for underwing stores. It entered service with 54 and 111 Squadrons in March 1955 and by

The famed RAF aerobatic display team of the late '50s, 'The Black Arrows', flew five Hunter F6s. These aircraft of No 111 Squadron were supplanted by the 'Blue Diamonds' team of 92 Squadron also flying Hunters, in 1961 (Brian Pymm).

1956 had replaced the Meteor 8 and Venom in some thirteen squadrons of the 2nd TAF and seven more in the UK. Some 365 Hunter F4s were built by Hawkers and were followed by 105 Armstrong Whitworth-built F5s fitted with the AW Sapphire engine.

The Hunter F6 saw a vast improvement in overall performance and was virtually a new aircraft, being fitted with the 10,000 lb thrust Avon 203 engine, all-flying tailplane and extended-chord dog-tooth wing. It first entered service with 74 Squadron in 1956 and in early November F6s and F5s based in Cyprus took part in the Suez Campaign. Altogether, some 383 F6s were supplied to the RAF and by 1958 the type equipped all RAF day fighter squadrons in Europe. In March that year 208 Squadron was re-formed with F6s and posted to the MEAF in Cyprus.

The Hunter FR10 was developed from the F6 and was produced as a Swift FR5 replacement for the 2nd TAF in Germany. The FR10 made its maiden flight on 7 November 1958 and began equipping 2 Squadron in 1960. It differed from the F6 in having three cameras in the nose and other internal equipment.

The F6 also formed the equipment of two famous Hunter aerobatic display teams, the 'Black Arrows' of 'Treble-One' Squadron, and the 'Blue Diamonds' of 92 Squadron. The 'Black Arrows' first appeared in April 1957 and quickly established themselves as one of the world's finest formation aerobatic teams. The highpoint of their two year career was probably the formation loop by 22 Hunters at the 1958 Farnborough Air Show. In 1961 the 'Blue Diamonds' assumed the mantle of the RAF's premier formation aerobatic team with its characteristic diamond nine formation. Now only the 'Blue Herons' aerobatic display team, with its four Hunter GA11s, use this famous British aircraft. The Blue Herons was formed by Airwork Services' pilots at RNAS Yeovilton in 1975 and is believed to be the first aerobatic team in the world in which civilians fly military aircraft.

The FG9 was a development of the F6 and was originally intended for service exclusively in the Middle East as a Venom replacement. Deliveries to the RAF began in October 1959 when 8 Squadron at Aden began re-equipping with the type. From 1962 Hunters began to be replaced in first-line service both at home and abroad by the Lightning F2 and the Canberra B(I)8. However, with the formation of Strike Command in April 1968, two FGA9 squadrons, 1 and 54, constituted the tactical support and strike force in the UK. The last FGA9s were finally withdrawn from first-line service when 8 Squadron returned from the Far East to disband at the end of 1971. A few Hunter FGA9s remained at Valley and Brawdy as trainers until replacement by the Hawk during 1980. Currently, the sole remaining Hunter T Mk 7s in RAF service provide an Integrated Flight Instrumentation System (IFIS) as a link between the Hawk advanced trainer and the operational Buccaneers at RAF Honington.

HAWKER SIDDELEY BUCCANEER

Type Two-seat strike and reconnaissance. **Crew** Two. **Manufacturers** Hawker Siddeley Aviation (formerly Blackburn Aircraft, now British Aerospace). **Power plant** (Late marks), Two Rolls-Royce Spey 101 turbofans. **Dimensions** (II) Span, 44 ft. Length, 63 ft 5 in. Height, 16 ft 3 in. **Weight** (II) Empty, 30,000 lb. Loaded, 62,000 lb. **Performance** Max speed, 645 mph at sea level. Service ceiling, in excess of 40,000 ft. Typical range, 2,300 miles. **Armament** (S1) Four 1,000 lb bombs or multi-sensor reconnaissance pack or 440 gallon tank in rotating bomb door.

The only new aircraft to survive from the infamous Defence White paper of 1957 was the Blackburn B103 which was originally known as the NA39. It was designed to an Admiralty requirement for a carrier-borne aircraft that was capable of delivering a nuclear weapon by penetrating enemy air space at very low level. The prototype flew for the first time on 30 April 1958 and it was later designated the Blackburn Buccaneer.

The S1 began equipping 801, the first operational Buccaneer

A Buccaneer S1 of 801 Squadron on the catapult of HMS Victorious.

A Hawker Siddeley Buccaneer S2 (distinguishable by the oval engine intakes) of 809 Squadron is catapulted from the deck of HMS Ark Royal *(Ray Mason).*

squadron, in July 1962 and this unit embarked in HMS *Ark Royal* on 20 February 1963. Some forty production Buccaneer S1s were ordered for the FAA and the type equipped a further two first-line units, 800 in HMS *Eagle* and 809 at Lossiemouth, before it was phased out of service from 1965 by the S2. This version differed from the S1 in having two Rolls-Royce Spey engines in place of the earlier Gyrons and much reduced fuel consumption. Its main distinguishing feature was the modification from circular engine intakes to an oval shape.

The S2 equipped four first-line squadrons of the FAA, one of its most memorable actions occuring in March 1967 when Buccaneers of 800 and 736 squadrons stationed at RNAS Brawdy took part in the *Torrey Canyon* oil tanker operation. The 84th and final S2 for the FAA was completed in December 1968, the year in which the RAF bought

Above *Messerschmitt Bf 109F Nightfighter being prepared for combat in 1942* (MBB).

Below *Messerschmitt Bf 110D used as an escort for Ju 52s in 1941* (MBB).

Above *North American P-51D Mustang 'Moose' landing during a display at the Mildenhall Air Fête in 1983* (Author).

Below *Republic P-47 Thunderbolt* (Author).

Above *Jaguar GR 1 of No 6 Squadron, RAF Coltishall, July 1980* (Author).

Below *Two Spitfire Mk IIs in company with a Gloster-built Hurricane I during 1942, all from the Empire CFS Hullavington* (Chas E. Brown).

Above *Spitfire Mk VB* (IWM).
Below *A BAe Harrier GR5, the latest production variant of this combat-proven type in RAF 'low visibility' markings* (British Aerospace).

this splendid aircraft to fill the gap left by successive cuts in defence spending. The S2 remained in service in HMS *Eagle* until it retired in 1972 and with 809 Squadron in *Ark Royal* until it was also retired, in late 1978.

The first of about 100 Buccaneers (42 built specially for the RAF and the remainder being ex-FAA aircraft) entered RAF service in October 1969 when 12 Squadron at Honington, Suffolk, began receiving the S2 for the maritime strike role. A year later 15 Squadron, also at Honington, began receiving the Buccaneer and in January 1971 was posted to Germany to become the first of its kind to serve with NATO. A second home-based Squadron, No 208, was formed at Honington in the overland strike role in July 1974. No 15 Squadron was later joined in RAF Germany by 16 Squadron.

The RAF S2A version (surplus FAA Buccaneers converted to S2A standard) are used in the overland tactical bombing role and the Martel-equipped S Mk 2B is used in the maritime strike and reconnaissance role. The Buccaneer is reportedly one of the most cost-effective aircraft ever built for tactical operations. It has earned the greatest admiration from American colleagues during Red Flag exercises at Nellis AFB, Nevada, where it has demonstrated its lo-lo-level characteristics to excellent advantage and much to the astonishment of American monitoring operators. In 1980, following a fatal crash during one of these exercises, twenty of the RAF's fifty Buccaneers were temporarily grounded after main spar cracks were discovered in the wings. Two aircraft were so badly affected that they could not be flown back from the USA.

The Buccaneer will gradually be replaced in RAF Germany by the Tornado GR1 and by the same aircraft in Strike Command during the early 1990s.

HAWKER SIDDELEY (BAe) HARRIER

Type V/STOL strike and reconnaissance fighter. **Crew** Pilot only. **Manufacturers** Hawker-Siddeley Aviation Ltd, Kingston-on-Thames and Dunsfold. **Power plant** One Rolls-Royce Pegasus 103 vectored thrust turbofan. **Dimensions** Span, 25 ft 3 in. Length, 45 ft 7¼ in. Height, 11 ft 3 in. **Weight** Empty, 12,400 lb. Loaded, 26,000 lb. **Performance** Max speed, 720 mph at 1,000 ft. Cruise, 560 mph at 20,000 ft. Combat radius, 260 miles. **Armament** Two 30 mm Aden cannon and up to 5,000 lb of external stores.

The Harrier V/STOL jet fighter more than any other aircraft has probably captured the imagination of the public and service alike. Despite political setbacks (in February 1965 the British Labour Government cancelled the P1154 supersonic version which would have been capable of Mach 2 at high altitudes) there seems no end to its potential in the highly competitive military market today. This was proved conclusively by its combat debut and subsequent success in the Falklands War (1982) when it became a fully fledged and proven dog-fighting aircraft in addition to its strike capability.

The world's first operational fixed-wing V/STOL aircraft began life as the P1127 which hovered in the air for the first time on 21 October 1960, using a vectored-thrust turbofan. On 13 March 1961 the P1127 Kestrel, as it was then called, made its first flight. The type was then evaluated by a British, American and West German composite squadron at RAF West Raynham, Norfolk from 15 October 1964 to 30 November 1965. These tripartite trials proved that the Kestrel was ideally suited for military purposes and led ultimately to an order for sixty Harrier GR1 single-seaters and ten Harrier T2 two-seaters. This was later increased to 135 Harriers.

The first of six development Harriers, which differed considerably from the earlier Kestrel, made its maiden flight on 31 August 1966 and the first true production aircraft flew on 28 December 1967. The type first equipped No 1 Squadron in June 1969 and began equipping 4 Squadron in RAF Germany in June 1970. By the beginning of 1972 Nos 3 and 20 Squadrons in RAF Germany had also been equipped with the GR1. All three squadrons operated from RAF Wildenrath near the Dutch border, only 150 miles west of the potential war zone. During the mid-1970s 20 Squadron's Harriers were re-allocated to Nos 3 and 4 Squadrons which moved to Gutersloh, only 75 miles from the East German border, during 1977. This forward redeployment

Harrier XV738, the first production standard aircraft, subsequently modified to GR3 standard and seen here in service with No 3 Squadron, launches a salvo from four SNEB rocket pods at a range in Sardinia (British Aerospace).

means that the Harriers can provide a more immediate response on day one of any future confrontation.

In the UK No 1 Squadron shares RAF Wittering with 233 Harrier OCU and is part of No 38 Group, Strike Command, which is earmarked for assignment to NATO in emergency. Late in 1975 Harriers of Strike Command were first deployed to Belize in central America to counter a threat by neighbouring Guatemala. In July 1977 six Harriers of No 1 Squadron resumed the border policing tasks in response to further build ups of Guatemalan forces.

In 1982 Harrier GR Mk 3s of No 1 Squadron played their part in the Falklands War alongside Sea Harriers of the Royal Navy. Fitted with AIM-9 Sidewinders (previously cleared for the AV-8As of the USMC and RN Sea Harriers only), the first GR3s flew a non-stop 9 hour 15 minute flight from St Mawgan, Cornwall to Wideawake Airfield on Ascension Island on 3 May. This record distance of 4,600 miles beat the previous record held by a single engine V/STOL aircraft of 3,500 miles from London to New York in the May 1969 *Daily Mail* Transatlantic Air Race.

On 18–20 May, after further GR3s had been delivered, pilots of No 1 Squadron flew to HMS *Hermes* and made their first deck landings on a carrier at sea. On their first training sortie Wing Commander Squire (CO of 1 Squadron) and Flight Lieutenant Glover were tasked to intercept an Argentine military Boeing 707 on a reconnaissance mission some 200 miles north-east of the Task Force.

From 20 May until 15 June, when the Argentine forces surrendered

The Harrier Mk I is known as the AV-8A in the US Marine Corps (British Aerospace).

at Port Stanley, RAF Harrier GR3s flew 126 operational sorties including support missions for the landings at San Carlos, Darwin and Goose Green. On 2 May Flight Lieutenant Paul Barton of No 1 Squadron shot down the first Argentinian aircraft of the war, a Mirage III. On 20 May the Harriers made an attack on Port Stanley airfield. During early June four replacement GR3s arrived, flying for 8½ hours directly from Ascension Island to the war zone. On 13 June Harrier GR3s made the first Paveway laser guided bomb attack in the Falklands with successful pinpoint attacks on two targets just before the Argentinian surrender was signed.

The Harrier GR1A was an updated version of the GR1 fitted with the 20,000 lb thrust Pegasus 102 engine. The GR3 differs in having a 21,500 lb thrust Pegasus 103 engine and Ferranti Laser Ranging and Marked Target Seeker fitted in an extended nose. The GR Mk 5/AV-8B now being developed jointly by BAe and McDonnell Douglas (also involved in joint supersonic Harrier design studies), is a higher-performance version with a Pegasus 11 Mk 105 engine, new wing with supercritical airfoil for improved lift and cruise characteristics. Epoxy composite materials are used in its construction and in other surfaces to save weight. A new inlet engine design permits greater engine thrust for V/STOL and STOL and more efficient cruise.

Modified from the UK built AV-8A, the prototype YAV-8B flew for the first time on 9 November 1978 at St Louis. Service entry with the US Marine Corps, which has a requirement for 328 AV-8Bs (including 28 two-seaters) began early in 1985. The Harrier II GR Mk 5 flew for the first time in May 1985. The RAF is to receive 62 aircraft and the first Mk 5s began equipping squadrons in RAF Germany in 1986.

The Harrier is truly a legend in its own lifetime.

HEINKEL He 219 *UHU* (OWL)

Type Night fighter. **Crew** Two/three. **Manufacturers** Ernst Heinkel AG.
Power plant Two 1,900 hp Daimler-Benz DB 603G engines. **Dimensions**
Span, 60 ft 8½ in. Length, 50 ft 11¾ in. Height, 13 ft 5½ in. **Weight** Empty,
24,692 lb. Loaded, 33,730 lb. **Performance** Max speed, 416 mph at 22,967 ft.
Absolute ceiling, 41,668 ft. **Armament** (He 219A-7) Eight cannon, two Mk
108 machine-guns in the wing roots, two Mk 103s and two MG151/20s in a
ventral tray and two upward firing 30 mm Mk 108s in Schrage Musik
installation aft of the cockpit.

Fortunately for the Allies, Germany's classic night fighter of the
Second World War, never reached volume production. First conceived in August 1940 as a private design venture for a daylight high-
speed fighter, bomber and torpedo strike aircraft, only 286 pre-
production and production aircraft were built, largely because the Air
Ministry had no need of the aircraft until the end of 1941 when RAF
area bombing of German cities was beginning to bite.

The Air Ministry asked Heinkel to produce the He 219 as a night
fighter but the design caused special problems. It embodied several
advanced features such as a nose wheel undercarriage, pressurized
cockpit and the first ejector seats to be used on an operational aircraft.
The He 219 was not ready for its first flight until 15 November 1942 but
test pilots at Rechlin realized the aircraft had immense potential and
the initial order for 100 was increased three-fold.

The *Luftwaffe* was so impressed that in early May 1943 it operated
the twenty *Versuchs* (prototypes) from Venlo, Holland as a special
trials unit. The first six sorties resulted in the destruction of twenty RAF
bombers including six high-speed Mosquitoes. When tested under
service conditions for the first time on the night of 11/12 June 1943,
Major Streib succeeded in shooting down five Lancaster bombers
during a single sortie.

The He 219 *Uhu* appeared in fifteen different versions but
production was slow. In December 1943 it was suggested that
production be discontinued solely in favour of Ju 88 production. This
was temporarily shelved, primarily because the *Uhu* was the only
German night fighter capable of matching the Mosquito in night
combat.

However, in May 1944 the *Uhu* was officially abandoned and only
195 were produced that year. In 1945 only a paltry 62 models were
built. The aircraft was so badly needed that another six He 219s were
assembled unofficially from spare components at service airfields.
The advancing Soviet Armies overran production facilities in Poland

Only 286 Heinkel He 219 Uhu *aircraft were built before the end of World War 2, but this German rival to the Mosquito nevertheless ranks as a classic fighter* (Jerry Scutts).

and eastern Germany and several of the hand-made prototypes, including a high altitude version, were destroyed by Allied bombing.

Many of the *Uhu*'s radar secrets were revealed after the war when 31 German night fighters, including a Heinkel He 219A-2, were brought to Britain for evaluation.

JUNKERS Ju 88G-7

Type Night fighter. **Crew** Four. **Manufacturers** Junkers Flugzeug and Motorenwerke AG. **Power plant** Two 1,880 hp Junkers Jumo 213E engines. **Dimensions** Span, 65 ft 7½ in. Length, 51 ft 1½ in. Height, 15 ft 11 in. **Weight** Empty, 20,062 lb. Loaded, 28,885 lb. **Performance** Max speed, 389 mph at 29,529 ft. Service ceiling, 32,810 ft. **Armament** Six MG151/20 cannon and one MG131 machine-gun.

By the summer of 1941 *Luftwaffe* General Kammhuber was developing Germany's night fighter arm with around 250 aircraft. None were new types but some, including the Ju 88, which was originally designed as a dive bomber, were to prove ideal in the night fighter role.

Nearly all the early German night fighters relied on ground control by Wurzburg radar to bring them to a visual sighting. The exceptions were four Junkers Ju 88s, equipped with the new Lichtenstein AI contact radar. At first these were disliked by German crews, who preferred to fly aircraft not fitted with the rudimentary external aerials because they were up to 25 mph faster than the Lichtenstein fighters.

Late in 1943 the Ju 88C series appeared but the type was never used in large numbers by the *Nachtjagdgeschwader*. One was fitted with Lichtenstein SN-2 radar and six cannon. The Ju 88C was followed on the production lines by a batch of Ju 88G-0 pre-production aircraft. These aircraft had four cannon and were fitted with improved FuG 220 Lichtenstein SN-2 radar. The Ju 88G-1 was put into production in the spring of 1944 and by August 1944 had been delivered to eight night fighter *Gruppes*.

The next production model was the Ju 88G-6a which was similar to the G-1 but was powered by two 1,700 hp BMW 801G engines. The Ju 88G-6b was fitted with additional radio equipment and had increased fuel capacity. It was also fitted with *Schrage Musik* ('Slanting Music'): two cannon mounted atop the fuselage, firing obliquely upwards and enabling night fighters to attack by closing in from behind and below. During the winter of 1943–44 the lethal SN-2/ *Schrage Musik* combination inflicted very heavy losses on RAF Bomber Command. On the night of 19/20 February during a raid on Leipzig, Bomber Command lost 78 out of 823 bombers. In the biggest night battle of the war, over Nuremburg on the night of 30/31 March 1944, the RAF lost 95 of its 795 attacking bombers, a further fifteen were written off in crashes and 59 were badly damaged.

The RAF gained a fortunate break when a Ju 88G-1 belonging to 7/ NJG2, landed at Woodbridge, Suffolk by mistake on 13 July 1944. The

A Junkers Ju 88G-6. This aircraft of 7 / Nachtjagdgeschwader 5 was flown to Switzerland by a defecting crew on 30 April 1945 (Stapfer).

Allies conducted a thorough evaluation of the type's FuG 200 Lichtenstein SN-2, and FuG 227 Flensburg radar, which homed on to emissions of the British 'Monica' tail warning radar. As a result this was quickly deleted from all Bomber Command aircraft and a new type of 'Window' was introduced to jam SN-2 radar.

The Ju 88G-6c differed from the G-6b in having two 1,750 hp Junkers Jumo 213A engines. The final production variant of the Ju 88G series was the -7, which was powered by two Jumo 213E engines. The Ju 88Ga carried FuG 220 Lichtenstein SN-2 radar and the G-7b had FuG 218 Neptun V radar with *Hirschgeweih* ('toasting fork') aerials or with the *Morgenstern* aerials enclosed in a wooden nose cone. A final ten Ju 88G-7c carried FuG 240 Berlin N-1s centimetric radar with a scanner enclosed in a wooden nose cone.

The Ju 88G finished the war as the primary night fighter in the *Nachtjagdgeschwader*. Among the many German night fighter aces who flew the Ju 88G was *Oberst* Helmut Lent, Kommodore of NJG3, with 102 victories at night. On the night of 3 March 1945 about 100 intruder aircraft attacked British defences. Twenty intruders were lost and the following night the last enemy aircraft to be brought down on British soil was a Ju 88G-6 from 13/NJG3 which crashed in Yorkshire.

Approximately 4,200 Ju 88 night fighters were produced.

LOCKHEED P-38 LIGHTNING

Type Pursuit, Long-range escort and (P-38M) night-fighter. **Crew** Pilot only; (P-38M) Two. **Manufacturers** Lockheed Aircraft Corporation, Burbank, California and Consolidated Vultee, Nashville, Tenn. **Specification (P-38L) — Power plant** Two Allison V-1710-111/113 engines. **Dimensions** Span, 52 ft. Length, 37 ft 10 in. Height, 9 ft 10 in. **Weight** Empty, 12,800 lb. Loaded, 21,600 lb. **Performance** Max speed, 414 mph at 25,000 ft, Service ceiling, 44,000 ft. **Armament** One 20 mm cannon, four .50 calibre machine-guns and provision for two 1,600 lb bombs.

The P-38 Lightning was one of the most easily recognizable fighters of the Second World War and together with the P-47 and P-51, formed the mainstay of the American fighter force in the USAAF from 1941–45. Originally designed in 1937 as a high altitude interceptor, the P-38 was already in mass production before the outbreak of hostilities. Production contracts had been placed before the first YP-38 made its maiden flight on 16 September 1940 and the first deliveries of the P-38D Lightning to the US Army Air Corps followed in August 1941. Beginning in late 1941 a few Lightning I versions with unsupercharged Allisons were supplied to the RAF but the majority were diverted to the USAAF after Pearl Harbor.

The first unit to operate the P-38 was the 342nd Composite Group operating from Icelandic bases. The first German aircraft shot down by a USAAF fighter occured on 14 August 1942 when two P-38s from the 27th Squadron of the 1st Fighter Group and a P-40, destroyed an FW200 Condor near Iceland.

The P-38's development as a long-range tactical fighter was delayed because of the prevailing belief that American heavy bombers could defend themselves on long daylight missions over Europe. By mid-1942 when heavy losses in the bomber groups made it obvious that long-range escort fighters would, after all, be required, the P-38F began to be deployed in large numbers in the European Theatre of Operations (ETO). Although slightly slower and less manoeuvrable than most single-engined fighters then in service, the Lightning's greater range made it an excellent escort fighter. It could take a great deal of punishment, lose one engine and still get its pilot home. The P-38J version appeared in August 1943 and was used mainly to accompany American heavy bombers of the 8th and 15th Air Forces on long-range missions from Britain and Italy respectively.

Beginning in November 1942 P-38s also saw large-scale service in North Africa and the Mediterranean theatre. In combat with the

Above *The Lockheed P-38 Lightning, one of the most easily recognizable fighters of the Second World War.*

Below *The Night Lightning saw service during the last weeks of the Pacific War and was heavily armed with machine guns, cannon and rockets (Lockheed).*

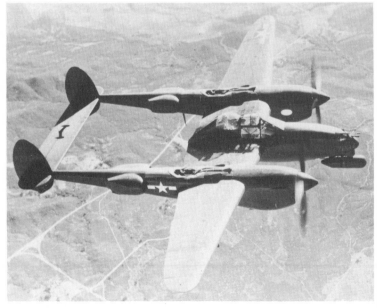

Luftwaffe for the first time the Lightning gave a good account of itself. Despite its drawbacks the P-38s devastating firepower and excellent rate of climb earned the respect of its German adversaries who referred to the P-38 as the 'Fork-Tailed Devil'.

The Japanese too, learned to hate the Lightning. The P-38 destroyed more Japanese aircraft than any other American aircraft and the two leading American aces, Major Richard Bong and Major Tom McGuire (40 and 38 kills respectively), flew P-38s in the Pacific theatre. In April 1943 Lightnings of the 339th Fighter Squadron succeeded in intercepting and shooting down the Mitsubishi transport carrying Admiral Yamamoto, mastermind of the Japanese attack on Pearl Harbor. The interception, 550 miles from their base at Guadalcanal, was made possible by the use of long-range drop tanks.

When production finally ended in 1945 almost 10,000 P-38s had been built.

LOCKHEED F-104 STARFIGHTER

Type F-104A/C, Day interceptor. F-104G, Multi-role fighter. F-104CF, strike-reconnaissance. F-104S, All-weather interceptor **Crew** Pilot only. **Manufacturers** Lockheed Aircraft Corp, Burbank, California. Also built under licence by NATO Consortium, Canadair (CF-104), Japan (F-104J) and Italy (F-104S). **Specification (F-104G) — Power plant** One General Electric J79. **Dimensions** Span, 21 ft 11 in. Length, 54 ft 9 in. Height, 13 ft 6 in. **Weight** Empty, 14,082 lb. Max loaded, 28,779 lb. **Performance** Max speed, 1,450 mph at 40,000 ft (Mach 2.2). Service ceiling, 58,000 ft. **Armament** (F-104S) One 20 mm M-61 Vulcan rotary cannon and two AIM-7 Sparrow III and two AIM-9 Sidewinder air-to-air missiles.

Conceived by USAF experience in Korea, the F-104 has been the principle fighter aircraft flown by fifteen different nations. In November 1952 Clarence 'Kelly' Johnson's famed 'Skunk Works' design group began creating the Model 83 and the first prototype rolled out of Lockheed's Burbank factory in 1953. Considered to be years ahead of its time observers noted its extremely small wing area and downward-ejecting seat. The XF-104 flew for the first time on 7 February 1954 fitted with a General Electric J65 Sapphire with afterburner.

The F-104A, which made its maiden flight ten days later, was fitted with a more powerful engine and blown flaps. On 27 April 1955 Mach 2 was achieved in a YF-104A for the first time. In its first year of service with the USAF in 1958 when it equipped Air Defense Command, the F-104A became the first operational interceptor capable of sustained Mach 2+ speeds and the first aircraft to hold World airspeed and altitude records simultaneously.

Only 170 F-104As were built. In 1960 they were withdrawn from ADC and issued to the Air National Guard although later some F-104As, fitted with the GE-19 engine, returned to first-line service. The F-104C fighter-bomber variant fitted with a refuelling probe was developed for service with Tactical Air Command. Deliveries to the 831st Air Division began on 16 October 1958 at George AFB. On 14 December 1959 an F-104C took the altitude record to 103,389 ft.

The F-104G, which flew for the first time on 5 October 1960, represented a complete re-design to meet the requirements laid down by the *Luftwaffe* for a tactical nuclear strike and reconnaissance aircraft. This model was also adopted by other NATO countries. Altogether, some 1,266 Gs were built, including 970 by the NATO consortium. Unfortunately, the F-104 suffered a high accident

F-104C Starfighters in formation. Note the refuelling probe on the aircraft second from the camera.

rate in NATO service. The Belgian Air Force lost 39 of its 100 Starfighters, the Dutch Air Force, 44 of its 138 Starfighters and by late 1982 the *Luftwaffe* had lost 252 of its 917 Starfighters. The Dutch later sold 53 Starfighters to Turkey and ten to Greece. Canadair was the other major Starfighter producer, building 310 F-104Gs and CF-104s. Mitsubishi built 207 F-104Js for the Japanese Self Defence Force.

The final version of the Starfighter was the F-104S, developed jointly by Lockheed and Fiat (Aeritalia). The F-104S, was an air-superiority fighter and received its designation 'S' from its two Sparrow air-to-air missiles. The first of two F-104S prototypes appeared in December 1966 and the first Fiat-built 'S' aircraft flew on 30 December 1968. Altogether, 205 F-104S aircraft were delivered to the *Aeronautica Militare Italiana*. The final Lockheed-built F-104, co-produced with Italy, left the factory in April 1968. The last Italian-produced F-104S was rolled out in March 1979 to take world-wide production of the Starfighter to 2,583.

Starfighter units in NATO have been or are being replaced by the Tornado and F-16A. In West Germany the Tornado is re-equipping all four F-104G wings in the *Luftwaffe* and all three F-104G/RF-104G wings in the *Marineflieger*. The Tornado is replacing the F-104G and RF-104G in the Italian Air Force, although the F-104S, which equips nine squadrons, will remain in service in the late 1980s. The F-16 has replaced F-104Gs and F-104Ds in Belgium, Holland and Norway. Some F-104Gs remain in service in Denmark, Greece and Turkey and the CF-104G equips three squadrons in 1 Canadian Air Group of the Canadian Armed Forces in West Germany.

MACCHI C.202/C.205

Type Fighter. **Crew** Pilot only. **Manufacturers** Aeronautica Macchi; Societa Italiana Ernesto Breda; SAI Ambrosini. **Power plant** One 1,075 hp Alfa Romeo RA1000 RC411 V-12 liquid-cooled engine. **Dimensions** Span, 34 ft 8½ in. Length, 29 ft 0½ in. Height, 11 ft 5¾ in. **Weight** Empty, 5,490 lb. Loaded, 6,459 lb. **Performance** Max speed, 370 mph at 19,685 ft. Service ceiling, 37,730 ft. **Armament** Two 12.7 mm and two 7.7 mm Breda-SAFAT machine-guns.

Soon after its introduction to the *Regia Aeronautica* in the late 1930s it was realized that the Macchi MC200 fighter would suffer with its low-powered 840 hp Fiat A74 engine. Macchi took steps to improve its design and performance by replacing the Fiat engine with a Daimler-Benz DB601A-1 and the prototype C.202 *Folgore* (Lightning) emerged. This aircraft flew for the first time on 10 August 1940.

Many component parts were based on the Macchi MC200 Saetta so tooling up for production was a fairly simple task. The *Folgore* retained its predecessor's twin Breda machine-guns in the nose and some versions housed two machine-guns in the wings but its cockpit was completely enclosed. Licence arrangements were made for Alfa Romeo to produce the Daimler-Benz engine and Breda commenced Folgore production late in 1940.

The type first entered service in July 1941 and its exceptional rate

Macchi Folgore with underwing guns (Stapfer).

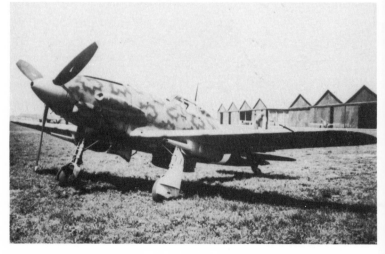

Macchi 202V Veltro Series III, MM92289. *Capitano Wilfredo Trevisini defected to Lausanne airfield, Switzerland in this aircraft on 3 March 1944* (Stapfer).

of climb and manoeuvrability helped achieve total dominance over the RAF Hurricanes and P-40s in the Western Desert.

On 19 April 1942 a converted *Folgore* fitted with the more powerful 1475 hp DB605A-1 engine flew for the first time. The new type was designated the C.205 *Veltro* (Greyhound) and first entered service with the *Regia Aeronautica* in July 1943. The *Veltro* was a pilots' aircraft although performance and armament was poor by Allied standards. Armament was later improved with the introduction of two 20 mm Mauser MG151/20 machine-guns in place of the two 7.7 mm wing guns.

Poor engine output was instrumental in limiting both *Folgore* and *Veltro* production. Alfa Romeo failed to keep up with demand for the *Folgore* and *Veltro* production was almost brought to a standstill by the lack of licence-built Fiat RA1050 RC58 Tifone engines. When the Italian armistice was signed in September 1943, only 1,500 (392 by Macchi) *Folgores* had been built, including a paltry 66 *Veltros*. Most of these and some C.205N-1 *Orione* (Orion) variants carried on with the Italian Co-Belligerent Air Force.

McDONNELL DOUGLAS F-4 PHANTOM II

Type All-weather fighter, ground-attack, interceptor and fighter-reconnaissance. **Crew** Two. **Manufacturers** McDonnell Douglas Aircraft Corporation, St Louis, Missouri. (RN/RAF versions) BAC (Now BAe) Preston; rear fuselage and fin/rudder assemblies. Short Brothers, Belfast, outer wing panels. **Power plant** (F-4E) Two General Electric J79-GE-17 turbojets. (RN/RAF versions) Two Rolls-Royce RB168-25R Spey 202 turbojets. **Dimensions** Span, 38 ft 5 in. Length, 57 ft 11 in. Height, 16 ft 3 in. **Weight** Empty, 31,000 lb. Loaded, 58,000 lb. **Performance** Max speed (F4-E) (clean) 910 mph at 1,000 ft. 1,500 mph at 40,000 ft. (Spey) 1,386 mph at 40,000 ft (Mach 2.1), 920 mph at 1,000 ft (Mach 1.5). Maximum range, 1,750 miles. Service ceiling 60,000 ft. **Armament** (FGI); Four Sparrow air-to-air radar-guided missiles and four Sidewinder air-to-air infra-red missiles. (FGR2): Eleven 1,000 lb free-fall or retarded bombs, 126 SNEB 68 mm armour-piercing rockets. One 20 mm Vulcan SUU 23 rotary cannon.

When the US Navy placed a letter of intent for a new shipboard fighter on 18 October 1954, few could have foreseen the multitude of roles this most successful of post-war fighters would fulfil. As early as 1955 changes in specification altered the Phantom's primary role from a twin-engined strike aircraft to that of a long-range, high-altitude interceptor. The XF4H-1 made its maiden flight on 27 May 1958 and delivery to the US Navy began in February 1960 for carrier trials. In all, 1,218 Phantom IIs have been supplied to the US Navy with a further 46 to the USMC.

The first Phantom to equip the USAF was the F-4C tactical fighter developed from the US Navy F-4B. The F-4C differed from the naval version in having dual controls, an inertial navigation system, J79-GE-15 turbojets and boom flight refueling as well as provision for a large external weapons load. Altogether, 583 F-4Cs were built and served with the USAF in a variety of roles including close-support, attack and air superiority.

The F-4D was developed from the F-4C and introduced improved weapons delivery systems. The type flew for the first time in December 1965 and began equipping the USAF in March 1966. In all, 843 F-4Ds were built and some equipped the air forces of Iran and the Republic of Korea.

The F-4E, which first flew on 30 June 1967, is a multi-role fighter designed for the close-support, interdiction and air-superiority roles. The type is fitted with a 20 mm Vulcan rotary cannon and in the

A Phantom F-4D of the 52nd Tactical Fighter Wing, based at Spangdaheim, West Germany.

intercept role can carry four or six AIM-7E plus four AIM-9D air-to-air missiles. Internally, the F-4E carries an additional fuselage fuel tank, improved fire-control and target guidance systems while leading-edge slats were retro-fitted to improve manoeuvrability. The F-4G or 'Wild Weasel' is a modified F-4E with highly sophisticated electronic warfare systems for defence-suppression purposes.

A grand total of 2,712 Phantoms have been delivered to the USAF, but the Phantom II also serves with eight foreign air forces including the *Luftwaffe* (F-4F and RF-4E), *Heyl Ha'Avir* (Israel) (RF-4E) and the Royal Air Force. In July 1964 the first British orders were placed with McDonnell Douglas for a deck-landing version of the F-4K Phantom

Phantom FG 1 (F–4K), XV588, of 892 Squadron, Fleet Air Arm, on the catapult of HMS Ark Royal *in March 1972.*

for the Royal Navy to replace the Sea Vixen. In June 1965 it was also decided to order it for the RAF under the designation F-4M after the cancellation of the HS1154. An initial contract was placed for two YF-4Ms and twenty F-4Ms and the first RAF Phantom made its maiden flight at St Louis on 17 February 1967. Further cuts in defence spending reduced the original order for 140 Phantoms for the Royal Navy to only 28 aircraft.

All aircraft were re-engined with Rolls-Royce Spey turbofans in place of the J79 turbojets and versions for the Royal Navy were fitted with a folding nose radome to fit RN hangar lifts, larger flaps, drooping

Messerschmitt Bf 109E–4 camouflaged for operations in North Africa (MPB).

two MG17 machine-guns and two more in the wings, were made to operational units. The C-2 introduced a fifth machine-gun in the nose, firing through the propeller hub. The Bf 109D-1 was fitted with a Daimler Benz DB600 engine and a three-blade propeller. Production began in 1937 but the D was soon replaced on the production lines by the end of 1938 by the E-1. This type flew for the first time in January 1939 and deliveries to first-line units began the following month. Major production was now shared between Arado, Erla, Fieseler and Focke-Wulf as well as the Bayerische Flugzeugwerke. The annexation of Austria in March 1938 led to Bf 109s being produced at Wiener Neustadt.

When war was declared in September 1939 *Luftwaffe* fighter units were equipped with just over a thousand Bf 109Es. After meeting ineffectual opposition in the early offensives against Poland and the Low Countries, only the French Dewoitine D520 posed a threat to the all-conquering 109E, known by its pilots as the 'Emil'. Ten squadrons of RAF Hurricanes in France were unable to outwit the superior tactics of the Bf 109 units and the survivors were withdrawn to southern England in May 1940. It was not until 27 May, over the beaches of Dunkirk, that the Bf 109 engaged in combat for the first time with its equal, the Spitfire.

Early in July 1940 the *Luftwaffe* began operations over southern England and Bf 109s renewed their combat with the Hurricane. The RAF realized that the latter aircraft was out-matched by the German fighter so it was switched to bomber interception, leaving the Spitfire to take on the 109s. It had always been intended to use the Bf 110 as a long-range bomber escort but this aircraft proved unable to defend itself. The 109 filled the role and for the first time its limited range was exposed by the defending RAF fighters. With an operational endurance of only some thirty minutes at most over southern England, bomber escort became very dangerous and Bf 109 losses mounted. Many leading German air commanders, Adolf Galland included, attributed the *Luftwaffe*'s defeat in the Battle of Britain to the German High Command's tactical misuse of the Bf 109E rather than any technical differences between it and the RAF fighters.

In combat, the 109E's greatest advantage over the Hurricane and Spitfire was the ability to perform negative-G manoeuvres on account of its fuel-injection system. The RAF fighters were equipped with conventional carburettors and their Merlin engines lost power in negative-g conditions. Like the Spitfire the Bf 109E had ground handling problems because of its narrow track landing gear and it tended to swing alarmingly on take-off and landing. Despite these and other problems, not least bad visibility from the cramped cockpit, the Bf 109E remained the *Luftwaffe*'s first-line fighter until 1941 when the Bf 109F entered service.

After the daylight offensive in the Battle of Britain, Hermann Goering, the *Luftwaffe* fighter chief, ordered that a *Staffel* from each *Jagdgeschwader* be converted for fighter-bomber operations. On 22 June 1941 Bf 109E fighter-bombers fitted with fragmentation bombs were used successfully against Soviet aircraft on the ground during the opening phase of Operation Barbarossa.

Among the 109E sub-types were the E-1, which led to the Bf 109T carrier-borne fighter, E-4 without engine cannon, the E-5 and E-6 reconnaissance fighters with wing cannon deleted and the E-Trop fitted with filters to help prevent sand and dust entering the engine. The E-4/Trop fighter saw service in the Middle East and was also used in Russia. The E-7/Z introduced the GM-1 nitrous oxide booster.

Altogether, some 34,000 Bf 109s were built.

MESSERSCHMITT Bf 110

Type Day and night fighter. **Crew** Two. **Manufacturers** Bayerische Flug-zeugwerke (later Messerschmitt AG). **Power plant** Two Daimler Benz DB601A. **Dimensions** Span, 53 ft 4¾ in. Length, 39 ft 8½ in. Height, 11 ft 6 in. **Weight** Empty, 9,920 lb. Loaded, 15,430 lb. **Performance** Max speed, 349 mph at 22,966 ft. Service ceiling, 32,800 ft. **Armament** Two 20 mm Oerlikon MG FF cannon and four Rheinmetall 7.92 mm MG15 machine-guns. (G-4) Two 30 mm Mk 108 and two 20 mm MG151 plus two MG151 in *Schrage Musik* installation.

Designed in 1934 as a *Zerstörer* (Destroyer), the Bf 110 was the most successful twin-engined fighter in service at the outbreak of World War Two. Although arriving too late to see service in the Spanish Civil War, it soon gained a reputation in the invasion of Poland, operating in the close support role. After a severe setback in the Battle of Britain, this versatile aircraft served the *Luftwaffe* as a highly effective fighter at night and was still in production in 1945.

The Bf 110V1 prototype flew for the first time on 12 May 1936 and further examples were tested in 1937. On 19 April 1938 the Bf 110B-0 made its maiden flight but few Bs were produced before the type was replaced on the production lines by the Bf 110C. It was this version which began equipping the *Luftwaffe* in quantity, beginning in February 1939. By the outbreak of war in September that year three I/Z (*Zerstörer*) *Gruppen* were equipped with about 195 Bf 110Cs. Operating as escorts for the bombers they helped destroy the token opposition put up by the high wing monoplanes of the Polish Air Force.

Bf 110s were equally successful during the *Blitzkrieg* in the west when the air forces of France, Holland and Belgium were over-whelmed. The Bf 110 finally met its match over southern England in 1940 when it joined in combat with RAF Spitfires and Hurricanes. These two fighters completely outclassed the twin-engined type and Bf 109s were detailed to 'escort the escorts'. However, there were too few single-engined fighters to spare, so the Bf 110s were forced to operate alone and literally fly around in defensive circles when attacked. The Bf 110 suffered large losses in the Battle of Britain and the last fighter-bomber raid was flown on 27 September 1940 when the *Luftwaffe* attacked Bristol. Bf 110s fighter bombers fought in the Middle East from late 1940 and in Russia from June 1941.

By June 1941 four of the five German night-fighter units were equipped with the Bf 110. With the failure of its intended replacement, the Me 210, the Bf 110G was put into production. The Bf 110G series had more powerful engines than earlier Bf 110 models. The most

Messerschmitt Bf 110G-4 night fighters during daylight operations over the Reich territory (Bundesarchiv).

widely used night-fighter variant was the Bf 110G-4, armed with two cannon and two machine-guns in the nose. The G-4/R8 variant also housed two 20 mm MG FF cannon in a *Schrage Musik* ('Slanting Music') installation behind the rear cockpit. By the end of 1942 the German night fighter force was equipped with 389 aircraft, of which about 300 were Bf 110s. Fitted with Lichtenstein airborne radar and heavily armed, they accounted for more Allied night bombers than any other type.

Throughout late 1943 and in early 1944 rocket-firing Bf 110s were used to break up American 8th Air Force formations flying daylight missions over the Reich. With the introduction of long-range American escort fighters such as the Mustang, Bf 110 losses again mounted and units were disbanded or re-equipped with the Me 410. By December 1944 only about 150 Bf 110 night-fighters remained in service. Many finished their days pressed into desperate service in the ground attack role at night and losses were very high.

MESSERSCHMITT Me 262

Type Fighter, fighter bomber. **Crew** Pilot only. **Manufacturers** Messerschmitt AG. **Power plant** Two Junkers Jumo 004B axial flow turbojets. **Dimensions** Span, 41 ft 0.⅛ in. Length, 34 ft 9½ in. Height, 12 ft 6¾ in. **Weight** Empty, 8,820 lb. Loaded, 14,938 lb. **Performance** Max speed, 536 mph at 22,880 ft (winter) (508 mph in summer). Service ceiling, 37,565 ft. **Armament** Four Rheinmetall Borsig Mk 108 30 mm cannon. One 500 kg bomb or two 250 kg bombs. Twelve 55 mm R4M rocket projectiles below each wing.

Although it was not the first jet propelled aircraft to fly, the Me 262 was probably the first jet fighter to enter service anywhere in the world: an incredible feat for an aircraft produced by a war economy beset with jet engine shortages and material problems.

Design work began in the autumn of 1938 and the original design was complete by June 1939. The prototype, which featured a tailwheel undercarriage, was available long before the Junkers turbojet engines were satisfactorily developed. The Me 262 made its initial flight in April 1941, powered by a single Jumo 210G piston engine mounted on the nose. It was not until July 1942 that the third prototype was flown with Jumo 004-0 jet engines. From the fifth aircraft onwards a nose-wheel type undercarriage was fitted.

By April 1944 thirteen pre-production Me 262A-0 models had been

The Me 262A-1a never realized its full potential as an interceptor fighter. This aircraft of III/JG7 was flown to Switzerland on 25 April 1945 (Stapfer).

The Me 262B-1a/U1 night fighter fitted with SN2 Lichtenstein radar (Stapfer).

completed and deliveries began to the *Luftwaffe* trials unit at Lechfeld, Bavaria. Further fighter development was interrupted in May by Adolf Hitler who insisted that the type carry bombs. Despite the political intervention, by far the most limiting effect on Me 262 production was the delay in mass-producing the Jumo 004 jet engine. Essential materials such as high-temperature resistant chromium and nickel for the compressor blades were scarce. Combustion chambers made of steel with a spray coating of aluminium proved so unreliable that the turbojets had a life of only 25 flying hours before replacement was necessary.

By D-Day 1944 only about thirty Me 262s had been delivered to the *Luftwaffe* and none were operational. Me 262A-2a *Sturmvogel* (Stormbird) fighter-bombers of Kommando Schenk, commanded by Major Wolfgang Schenk, first saw action after 20 July 1944 in support of the German ground forces in France. The Me 262A-1a *Schwalbe* (Swallow) fighter entered operational service on 3 October 1944 with Kommando Nowotny, commanded by Major Walter Nowotny, the Austrian fighter ace (KIA 8 November 1944).

In the first month Nowotny's unit claimed 22 victories during operations against American daylight bomber formations despite having only three to four jets available on any one day. The Me 262's operational performance was limited by altitude and performance restrictions imposed by their turbojets. The chief drawbacks were a low rate of acceleration and a tendency to flame out at altitude. The throttle had to be handled very carefully because the fuel flow was not easy to control. Re-starting in the air was extremely difficult.

Despite an excellent rate of climb, high speed and heavy firepower, the Me 262 arrived too late and in too few numbers to influence the outcome of the war. Little more than 200 of the 1,433 Me 262 jet fighters built actually saw service with the *Luftwaffe*.

MITSUBISHI A6M ZERO-SEN

Type Carrier-borne fighter. **Crew** Pilot only. **Manufacturers** Mitsubishi Jukogyo KK. Nakajima Hikoki. **Power plant** (A6M2) One 925 hp Nakajima NK1C Sakae 12. **Dimensions** Span, 39 ft 4½ in. Length, 29 ft 9 in. Height, 9 ft 7 in. **Weight** Empty, 3,704 lb. Loaded, 5,313 lb. **Performance** Max speed, 316 mph. Service ceiling, 33,790 ft. **Armament** Two 20 mm Type 99 cannon and two 7.7 mm Type 97 machine-guns. Provisions for two 66 lb bombs.

This most famous of Japanese combat aircraft was designed in 1937 by Jiro Horikoshi to meet an exacting specification laid down by the Imperial Japanese Navy to replace its Mitsubishi A5M Claude carrier-fighter. The prototype Zero flew for the first time in April 1939 and the type entered production as the A6M2 Reisen in 1940. As this corresponded to the year 5700 in the Japanese calendar, the type became popularly known as the Zero-Sen (Type 00 fighter).

Its first combat test occurred in July 1940 during the Sino-Japanese War where it was sent for trials under operational conditions. The Zero out-performed all other types in combat used in China, including the Curtiss P-40s of Claire Chennault's Flying Tigers American volunteer force.

More than 400 Zeros had been delivered to the Imperial Japanese Navy by the time of the attack on Pearl Harbor in December 1941. The US soon discovered to its cost that the highly manoeuvrable and heavily armed A6M2 Zero was superior to the Grumman F4F Wildcat and even to its land-based fighters. However, although the Zero had a higher top speed and was faster in the climb than any Allied aircraft, it had its drawbacks. The Zero was poorly armoured and in combat its light alloy construction tended to catch fire easily. US Navy F4F pilots soon learned to avoid close-in dog-fights with the Zero and used their superior diving speeds instead. They soon found that diving through Zero formations from on high and firing all the while brought results.

The A6M2 Zero reigned supreme in the Pacific until the Battle of Midway in June 1942. During 1942–43 F4U Corsairs and F6F Hellcats of the US carrier-fleet achieved air superiority. Mitsubishi responded in August 1943 with the A6M5 version with a stronger wing to permit it to dive faster. The A6M5b introduced an armoured windscreen and fuel tank fire extinguishers.

On 19 June 1944 in the Battle of the Philippine Sea, A6M5a and 5b fighters were decimated by the F6F. In all, the Japanese lost 315 land-based and carrier-borne aircraft in what became known as the 'Marianas Turkey Shoot'. US losses were just 23 aircraft. As a result the Imperial Navy issued an urgent requirement for a greatly improved

Mitsubishi Zero-Sen.

Zero. The Mitsubishi A6M5c introduced armour for the pilot, increased fuel tankage and heavier calibre guns. These innovations increased weight but it was not until the end of 1944, when the Sakae 31 1,130 hp engine was introduced, that performance was improved upon.

By October 1944 the Imperial Navy had lost its aircraft carriers and the Zero finished the war as a land-based fighter. Few experienced Japanese fighter pilots remained to fly them so they were used on 'Kamikaze' suicide missions against Allied shipping.

The A6M5 was the largest single quantity Zero produced and by the end of the war some 10,937 Zeros of all types, including 6,217 by Nakajima, had been built.

NORTH AMERICAN P-51 MUSTANG

Type Fighter-reconnaissance, fighter-bomber. **Crew** Pilot only. **Manufacturers** North American Aviation, Inglewood, California and Dallas, Texas. (200 Mustangs built under licence 1945–48 by Commonwealth Aircraft of Australia and 1967–68 Cavalier re-entered production with new or re-manufactured models including turbo-prop and Enforcer versions). **Specification (P-51D/K) — Power plant** One 1,490 hp Allison V-1650-79 or one 1,680 hp Packard Merlin V-1650-7. **Dimensions** Span, 37 ft. Length, 32 ft 3 in. Height, 12 ft 2 in. **Weight** Empty, 7,125 lb. Loaded, 11,600 lb. **Performance** Max speed, 437 mph at 25,000 ft. Range (normal), 950 miles; (maximum) 1,170 miles. Service ceiling, 41,900 ft. **Armament** Six .50 in machine-guns and provision for 1,000 lb of bombs.

The P-51 Mustang was designed from the outset to meet British requirements as a long-range wing mate for the Spitfire and Hurricane after North American Aviation was approached by the British Purchasing Commission in April 1940 to produce the Curtiss P-40. North American's suggestion that they build a brand new and infinitely superior fighter instead was accepted but a 120-day limit for the construction of a prototype was imposed. Undeterred, North American succeeded in delivering it in just 117 days. The prototype NA-73X flew for the first time on 26 October 1940 and the first production model for the RAF made its maiden flight on 1 May 1941.

The first of 620 Mustang Is for the RAF reached Britain in October 1941 and began equipping 2 Squadron at Sawbridgeworth in April 1942. However, it soon became apparent that the Allison powerplant would not perform at high altitudes and it was decided to operate the Mustang in the armed tactical reconnaissance role instead of using it as an interceptor. Even so, a speed of almost 3C0 mph at 8,000 ft made the Mustang ideal for ground attack and tactical reconnaissance. The type replaced the Curtiss Tomahawk in eleven UK-based Army Co-Operation squadrons and provided the equipment of twelve others. In August 1942 photo-reconnaissance Mustangs photographed German defence dispositions around Dieppe prior to the famous commando raid and in October were the first RAF single-engined fighters to overfly Germany. The Mk I was followed in RAF service by 150 Mk 1As and fifty Mk IIs.

In 1942 Lieutenant Colonel Thomas Hitchcock (later killed flying a Mustang), the US military attaché in London, encouraged by the Ambassador, J. G. Winant, suggested that the Mustang be developed

P-51B, probably of the 357th Fighter Group, 9th Air Force in England in 1944.

as a long-range fighter fitted with the Rolls-Royce Merlin engine. Accordingly, four Allison-engined aircraft were converted to Mustang Xs with Merlin 61 engines which produced a top speed of 400 mph at 30,000 ft. At the same time North American began fitting the Packard-built Merlin to the P-51B. Planners in the AAF saw the Mustang as a tactical fighter so the first deliveries of P-51Bs in November 1943 were assigned to three groups of the tactical 9th Air Force at the expense of 8th Fighter Command, whose need for a long-range escort fighter was critical. On 1 December 1943 P-51Bs of the 354th Fighter Group flew their first mission, a sweep over Belgium. The first escort mission for the bombers was flown on 5 December.

A compromise was reached between the 8th and 9th Air Forces and the first 8th Air Force unit to receive the P-51B was the 357th Fighter Group, stationed at Raydon, Essex. They flew their first escort mission on 11 February 1944. In March 1944 P-51Bs flew to Berlin

Mustang I, AG633, of 2 Squadron RAF (Imperial War Museum).

and back for the first time. From thenceforth the Mustang saw widespread use as an escort fighter on long-penetration raids deep into Germany. The Mustang's range of 2,080 miles, achieved by the use of wing drop tanks, was far in excess of that available in other fighters of the day. By the end of the war the P-51 equipped all but one of the 8th Air Force fighter groups.

The P-51B was followed by 1,750 P-51C variants which were similar but had increased internal fuel capacity and a British-designed Malcolm bulged sliding hood. The Mustang III (British equivalent to the P-51B/C) did not enter service with the RAF until February 1944 when it began equipping 19 Squadron at Ford. The first 250 ordered had the older, hinged cockpit canopy. With a maximum speed of 442 mph at 24,500 ft it was more than a match for German propeller-driven fighters in 1944 and could operate far over the continent with the aid of drop tanks. Mustang IIIs continued to escort medium and heavy bombers over the continent in 1944 and later crossed to France with the 2nd Tactical Air Force to act as fighter-bombers.

Mustang IIIs and IVs equipped eighteen squadrons of the RAF in the UK and 2nd TAF and six squadrons in the Mediterranean theatre. Mustangs of 12 Group participated in the fight against the V1 and in three months ending 5 September 1944 had destroyed 232 Doodle-bugs. At the end of 1944 Mustangs of the 2nd TAF were withdrawn and rejoined Fighter Command but Mustangs of 11 and 13 Groups continued to escort US 8th Air Force daylight raids from the UK until the end of the war. Over 900 Mk IIIs and almost 9,000 Mk IVs entered service with the RAF and some were still serving with Fighter Command as late as November 1946.

The P-51D introduced a streamlined bubble (teardrop) canopy with a lowered rear decking and a change from four machine-guns to six. Later, a dorsal fin fairing was added. The P-51D was the most successful of all the Mustang models and was built in greater quantity than any other variant. Altogether, some 7,956 'D's were built and the type first saw service in Europe in 1944 with the USAAF and RAF (as the Mustang IV).

The P-51D also saw escort duty in the Pacific. In February 1945 P-51Ds flying from Iwo Jima escorted B-29s to attack Japan. On 7 April P-51Ds penetrated Tokyo airspace for the first time. A few P-51H models reached the Pacific before the end of the War and served operationally. This was the fastest of all Mustangs, having a top speed of 487 mph.

Post-war, the Mustang served with at least 55 air forces. Some served with Strategic Air Command until 1949 and the P-51K was withdrawn from service in 1951. Altogether, 15,586 versions of this remarkable aircraft were built.

NORTH AMERICAN F-86 SABRE

Type Fighter-bomber and all-weather interceptor fighter. **Crew** Pilot only. **Manufacturers** North American Aviation Inc, Inglewood, California and Columbus, Ohio. Sub-contracted by Canadair Ltd, Montreal, Canada. Societa per Azioni Fiat, Turin, Italy. **Specification (F-86A) — Power plant** One 5,200 lb thrust General Electric J-47 GE-13. **Dimensions** Span, 37 ft 1 in. Length, 37 ft 6 in. Height, 14 ft 8 in. **Weight** Empty, 10,495 lb. Loaded, 16,357 lb. **Performance** Max speed, 675 mph at 2,500 feet. Service ceiling, 48,300 ft. **Armament** Six .50 calibre machine-guns in nose, two 1,000 lb bombs or sixteen .5 in rocket projectiles.

The F-86 Sabre was the first transonic, swept wing jet fighter to see service in the West and the only United Nations fighter capable of meeting the MiG-15 on equal terms during the Korean War of 1950–53.

The straight wing XJF-1 flew for the first time on 27 November 1946 but the results of German wartime research into swept wings led to a 35° sweep angle being adopted for the XP-86. This aircraft made its inaugural flight on 1 October 1947 and the following spring it exceeded Mach 1, in a shallow dive, for the first time. The P-86A flew for the first time on 18 May 1948 and the following month the type was redesignated F-86A. Service deliveries began in December 1948 and the first unit to be fully equipped was the 1st Fighter Group at March Air Force Base, California in March 1949. That year a TG-190 (J57) engined YF-86D broke the world speed record at 671 mph.

The first unit to use the F-86A in Korea was the 4th Fighter-Interceptor Wing. Sabres from this wing joined in combat with the MiG 15 for the first time on 17 December 1950, shooting down four of the enemy. However, the MiG later proved to have the edge over the F-86A in climb and altitude performance. At transonic speed in a dive the F-86 tended to nose up and if the dive continued below 25,000 ft, it would begin to roll. These shortcomings were largely eliminated in the F-86E, which introduced a 'flying tail', power-operated controls and a slatted wing. In Korea pilots reported that intermittent opening of the wing slats caused them gun sighting problems during combat. The wing slats were deleted on the F-86F version which appeared in 1952. A new wing leading edge, extended by nine inches, was developed to improve manoeuvrability at high altitudes.

The F-86E-6 (CL-13), built by Canadair, was supplied to the USAF fitted with the General Electric J47-GE-13 turbojet. Altogether, some 1,815 CL-13s were produced through six marks by Canadair, including 430 J-47 engined Mk 2s and Mk 4s for the RAF. The RAF

Background photograph *North American F-86H Sabre with drop tanks.*

Inset *F-86K Sabres of the Royal Netherlands Air Force in May 1963.*

had no swept-wing fighters while the Meteor had proved unequal in combat with the MiG-15 in Korea. The 1952 air exercises, during which 'enemy' USAF Sabres completely outclassed defending Meteors of Fighter Command, and the worsening Cold War situation in Europe, prompted Britain to equip two squadrons in Fighter Command and ten squadrons of the 2nd TAF in Germany. By the end of 1953 all the Sabres in RAF service in Germany had been replaced by Hunters. The Mk 6 (CL-13B), powered by the Avro Canada Orenda 14 turbojet, was produced for the RCAF and SAAF.

During March 1951 deliveries of the F-86D all-weather collision-course interceptor fighter to the US Air Defence Command had begun. The 'Sabre Dog', as it was known, was armed with 24 2.75 in rockets. Its most significant feature was a reconfigured nose which housed a radar scanner above the engine intake. Altogether, 2,504 F-86D's were built. Some were subsequently converted to F-86L standard with increased span, extended and slotted leading edges and updated electronic equipment. The F-86K, which re-introduced four 20 mm cannon in place of the earlier rocket projectiles, was intended for service with NATO air forces. A total of 341 F-86Ks were built by North American and production also took place in Italy.

The F-86H, which flew for the first time on 30 April 1953, was the final production version of the Sabre for the USAF. Four 20 mm cannon replaced the six machine-guns in the nose and it had increased span, length and a deeper fuselage. By August 1955 473 had been produced by North American at Columbus. Altogether, some 9,502 Sabres were built by North American, Canadair, Mitsubishi and Societa per Azioni Fiat.

PANAVIA TORNADO GR Mk 1

Type Multi-role combat aircraft. **Crew** Two. **Manufacturers** Panavia Aircraft GmbH, Munich, West Germany; British Aerospace (42½%); Messerschmitt-Bolkow-Blohm (42½%) and Aeritalia (15%). **Power plant** Two 8,500 lb dry and 15,000 lb reheat Turbo-Union (A consortium consisting of Rolls-Royce, MTU and Fiat) RB 199-34R-4 Mk 101 turbo-fans. **Dimensions** Span (max) 45 ft 8 in. Length, 54 ft 9½ in. Height, 18 ft 8½ in. **Weight** Empty, 28,000 lb. Loaded, 55,000 lb. **Performance** Max speed 840 mph at 500 ft (Mach 1.1); 1,385 mph at 36,090 ft (Mach 2.1). **Armament** Two 27 mm Mauser cannon with 125 rpg and various ordnance combinations on seven (three fixed and four swivelling) external stores stations.

In 1969 Aeritalia of Italy, MBB of West Germany and British Aircraft Corporation (now British Aerospace), combined to form a consortium, known as Panavia, to build the Tornado multi-role combat aircraft (MRCA). There is a planned tri-national requirement for 809 aircraft to meet the needs of the RAF, the West German *Luftwaffe* (202 aircraft) and *Marineflieger* and the Italian Air Force. The RAF will procure a total of 385 aircraft including 165 F Mk 2 Air Defence Variant (ADV).

The first prototype Tornado made its maiden flight from Manching in West Germany on 14 August 1974 and a further eight prototypes

Tornado of the Marineflieger *normally armed with Komoran anti-ship missiles* (Author).

plus six pre-production aircraft had flown by 1981. On 21 January that year the Tri-National Tornado Training establishment was formally opened at RAF Cottesmore. Formation of the first all-RAF Tornado unit began at RAF Honington at the end of June with the arrival of the first Tornadoes of the Tornado Weapons Conversion Unit (TWCU). The unit is designed to give each pilot 32 hours in-combat training after an initial course at the Tri-National Tornado Training establishment at Cottesmore. In December 1981 the Tornado GR1 made its operational debut in Exercise 'Mallet Blow'.

The GR Mk 1 Interdiction and Strike (IDS) version first entered RAF service with No 9 Squadron at Honington on 9 June 1982. On 10 November 1982 one of the squadron's GR Mk 1s flew non-stop to Cyprus and back, a distance of 4,300 miles, refuelled in flight by Victor and Buccaneer tanker aircraft. No 9 Squadron's GR Mk 1s were followed into squadron service by 617 'Dambusters' Squadron at RAF Marham. In November 1984 Tornadoes from this squadron, supported by Victor K Mk 2s, participated in the US Strategic Air Command Bombing Competition, 'Giant Voice' at Ellsworth AFB, South Dakota. The 'Dambusters' took first and third place in the John C. Meyer Trophy, first and second in the Curtis LeMay Bombing Trophy and second and sixth place in the Mathis Trophy.

The Tornado GR Mk 1 has replaced Strike Command's Vulcans and Canberras in the UK. Beginning in February 1984, when 15 Squadron phased out its Buccaneers at Laarbruch, the Tornado had, by 1986, replaced seven squadrons of Buccaneers and Jaguars in RAF Germany. The Tornado GR Mk 1 is also destined to replace Strike Command Buccaneers in the early 1990s.

REPUBLIC P-47 THUNDERBOLT

Type Fighter, Fighter-bomber. **Crew** Pilot only. **Manufacturers** Republic Aviation Corp, Long Island, New York and Evansville, Indiana. Curtiss-Wright Corp, Buffalo, New York. **Specification (P-47D-25) — Power plant** One 2,300hp Pratt & Whitney Double Wasp R-2800-59. **Dimensions** Span, 40 ft 9 in. Length, 36 ft 1 in. Height, 14 ft 2 in. **Weight** Empty, 10,000 lb. Loaded, 19,400 lb. **Performance** Max speed, 428 mph at 30,000 ft. Service ceiling, 42,000 ft. **Armament** Eight .50 calibre machine-guns and provision for 2,000 lb of bombs below wings.

Designed originally as a strategic escort for deep penetration B-17s and B-24s over Europe in World War Two, the P-47 also served with distinction in the Pacific. The Prototype XP-47B flew for the first time on 6 May 1941 and deliveries of the P-47B began on 18 March 1942. Early models were known as 'Razorbacks' because of their raised

A Thunderbolt II of 30 Squadron RAF operating from Burma in 1945 (IWM).

rear fuselage leading to the framed cockpit hood. The first P-47Ds retained this canopy but from P-47D-25 on, Thunderbolts were fitted with a 'tear drop' moulded cockpit hood for improved rearward vision. Altogether, some 12,602 'D's were built.

By February 1943 both the 56th and 78th Fighter Groups of the 8th Air Force in England were operational on the P-47C and P-47D. Known alternatively as the 'Flying Milk Bottle' because of its shape and 'Jug' (for Juggernaut) because of its ability to outdive any other fighter, the P-47 soon gained the healthy respect of its pilots. Both the 56th and 78th flew their inaugural mission on 13 April 1943. The P-47s flew their first escort mission on 4 May 1943 when the 56th accompanied B-17s to Antwerp. On 28 July 1943 the 56th and 78th Fighter Groups carried unpressurized 200-gallon ferry tanks below the centre fuselage for the first time. After early teething troubles the P-47s value as a long-range escort was proved when two 150-gallon drop tanks were fitted below the wings to enable the P-47 to fly all the way to the target.

The 56th FG was unique in the 8th AF, choosing to retain its P-47s until the end of hostilities. Many famous aces served with this unit including its CO, Colonel Hubert Zemke (17¾ confirmed kills in the air), Major Gerald W. Johnson (with eighteen confirmed kills) and the top scoring fighter aces, Colonel Francis 'Gabby' Gabreski (who was the leading ace in the ETO with 28 victories and 2½ strafing credits) and Major Robert Johnson (28 aerial victories).

Although the Thunderbolt did not enter service with the RAF until September 1944 it distinguished itself during its exclusive service with Air Command, South East Asia in the fight against the Japanese. The Thunderbolt I was equivalent to the P-47B in USAAF service. The Thunderbolt II was the most widely used version in RAF service and was equivalent to the P-47D-25. Altogether, some 830 Thunderbolts served with sixteen RAF squadrons in Burma up until VJ-Day.

The final Thunderbolt models were the P-47M, of which 130 were built by 1945, and the P-47N, built solely for the Pacific Theatre. It had an 18 inch greater span than the P-47M to accommodate two 93-gallon tanks in addition to two drop tanks. With internal fuselage tanks and a 100-gallon belly drop tank, the P-47N had a range of 2,350 miles. Nearing the end of the war P-47Ns flew escort for the B-29s bombing targets in Japan.

By August 1945 P-47s had flown on every front destroying over 7,000 enemy aircraft on the ground and in the air. Altogether, 15,660 Thunderbolts were built and the last were phased out of service in 1955.

REPUBLIC F-105 THUNDERCHIEF

Type All-weather strike-fighter. **Crew** Pilot only. **Manufacturers** Republic Aviation Corp (now Fairchild Republic Company), Farmingdale, Long Island, New York. **Specification (F-105G) — Power Plant** One Pratt & Whitney J75-19W turbojet. **Dimensions** Span, 34 ft 11¼ in. Length, 69 ft 7½ in. Height, 20 ft 2 in. **Weight** Empty, 28,393 lb. Loaded, 54,000 lb. **Performance** Max speed, 1,480 mph (Mach 2.25). Service ceiling, 52,000 ft. **Armament** One 20 mm Vulcan M-61 rotary cannon. Internal bay for up to 8,000 lb ordnance and five pylons for additional 6,000 lb.

The 'Thud' as it was known was designed as a successor to the F-84F and was the largest single-seat, single engine combat aircraft in history.

On its first flight on 22 October 1955 the YF-105A, fitted with its Pratt & Whitney J57 engine, exceeded the speed of sound. The F-105B, which flew for the first time on 26 May 1956, was fitted with a J75-P-5 turbojet and was intended primarily for day operations. Only 75 F-105Bs were built and the type became operational with the US Tactical Air Command in January 1959. These were followed by 600 F-105D models. The 'D', which was flown for the first time on 9 June 1959, introduced a NASARR monopulse radar for use in both high and

F-105 Thunderchief of the USAF (USAF).

low-level missions and doppler navigation for night or bad weather operations. By the early 1960s the F-105D had become the primary strike-fighter with TAC and USAFE.

Production of the F-105 ceased in 1965 with the twin-seat F model but about 350 F-105Ds were rebuilt during the Vietnam War and some were modified to carry the T-Stick II system to improve all-weather bombing and blind-attack. About thirty Fs were converted to F-105G 'Wild Weasel' ECM attackers and during 1979–80 some were transferred to the Air National Guard and Air Force Reserve. Typical armament consisted of four Shrike missiles or two Standard ARMs.

ROYAL AIRCRAFT FACTORY
SE5a

Type Fighter. **Crew** Pilot only. **Manufacturers** Royal Aircraft Factory, Farnborough, Hampshire. **Power plant** One 200 hp or 220 hp Hispano-Suiza, 200 hp Wolseley W.4A Viper, 200 hp Wolseley Adder, or 200 hp Sunbeam Arab engine. **Dimensions** Span 26 ft 7½ in. Length 20 ft 11 in. **Weight** Loaded, 2,048 lb. **Performance** Max speed, 132 mph at 6,500 ft. Climb, 765 ft/min. Service ceiling, 20,000 ft. **Armament** One fixed, synchronized forward firing Vickers machine-gun and one Lewis machine-gun on a Foster mounting above the top wing. Provision for four 25 lb Cooper bombs under the wings.

The SE5a, developed from the SE (Scout Experimental) 5, was one of the finest single-seat fighters of the First World War and the favourite

This SE 5a of the Shuttleworth collection was originally built in 1918 by Wolseley Motors, Birmingham (Author).

mount of many British aces. One exception was Captain Albert Ball who flew the prototype SE5 in November 1916. He claimed the large celluloid windscreen impaired vision and he later had his own SE5 modified. Ironically, Ball was killed in an SE5 on 7 May 1917. His Squadron, No 56, was the first to receive the SE5, at London Colney, Hertfordshire, on 13 March 1917. Next month 56 Squadron was posted to France and became the first of fourteen squadrons to use the type on the Western Front. Deliveries of the SE5a began in June 1917 and eventually the type equipped 24 squadrons of the RFC and RAF in France, Palestine, Macedonia, Mesopotamia and the United Kingdom. It also equipped one squadron of the Australian Flying Corps and two squadrons of the US Air Service.

The SE5a was a very powerful and robust fighter which owed its combat success to a combination of speed and its stability as a gun platform. Among the most famous pilots who flew the SE5a were Major Edward 'Mick' Mannock VC and Major James McCudden VC. In March 1918 Mannock became a Flight Commander in the newly formed 74 'Tiger' Squadron equipped with the SE5a and in his three months with the unit added 36 kills to his previous score of 23 victories. Mannock was killed on 26 July 1918 when a German rifleman's bullet hit his petrol tank, but his confirmed total of 73 victories remained unbeaten by any other British ace during World War One. Major McCudden's total of 57 victories made him the fourth highest British ace by the end of the conflict. In six months of fighting with 56 Squadron he raised the score from seven on DH2s to around 57 on SE5a's flying as Flight Commander. Sadly, he was killed in a flying accident in France on 9 July 1918.

A total of 5,205 machines (SE5/SE5a) were built. Plans for a further 1,000 SE5a aircraft to be built by the Curtiss Company in America were cancelled after the cessation of hostilities.

SEPECAT JAGUAR

Type All-weather attack aircraft. **Crew** Pilot only. **Manufacturers** SEPECAT consortium formed by BAC (now British Aerospace) and Dassault-Breguet, France. **Power plant** Two Rolls-Royce/Turbomeca Adour turbofans. **Dimensions** Span, 28 ft 6 in. Length, 50 ft 11 in. Height, 16 ft 1½ in. **Weight** Empty, 15,000 lb. Loaded, 34,000 lb. **Performance** Max speed, 1,055 mph. Climb and ceiling, classified. **Armament** (A,E) Two 30 mm DEFA cannon (GR1), Two 30 mm Aden cannon. Five pylons for external stores.

In 1966 Breguet Aviation (later Dassault-Breguet) and British Aircraft Corporation (now British Aerospace), formed an Anglo-French company called *Société Européene de Production de L'Avion* (SEPECAT) specifically to produce the Jaguar all-weather strike fighter/dual operational trainer for both the RAF and the *Armée de l'Air*.

The first of eight prototypes was flown on 8 September 1968 and the first production Jaguar S for the UK was flown on 11 October 1972. No 226 OCU at Lossiemouth received the first S (GR Mk 1) in September 1973. The first operational unit to receive the aircraft was 54 Squadron at Coltishall, Norfolk, on 9 August 1974. This squadron

Jaguar of the French Air Force (Author).

was joined by 6 Squadron at the same station on 6 November 1974. By the beginning of 1978 all 202 ordered for the RAF had been delivered and equip eight fully operational Jaguar squadrons: 6, 54 and 41 at Coltishall, 14, 17, 20 and 31 and 2 Squadrons at Bruggen and Laarbruch respectively in Germany. (Nos 2 and 41 Squadrons operate in the reconnaissance role).

Some 35 Jaguars in RAF service are T2 advanced operational trainers. British Jaguars differ from the French A version in having Marconi-Elliott digital/inertial navigation and weapon aiming system, Smith's electronic head-up display (HUD) and Ferranti laser range-finder and marked target seeker in a specially modified nose. The *Armée de l'Air* ordered 200 Jaguars (including forty two-seat E. versions). From 1978 all RAF Jaguars underwent an engine retrofit programme with the uprated Adour 804 used in the Jaguar International replacing the Adour 102.

SOPWITH CAMEL

Type Fighting scout. **Crew** Pilot only. **Manufacturers** Sopwith Aviation, Kingston-Upon-Thames. Sub-contracted by Boulton & Paul, Norwich; British Caudron, Cricklewood; Clayton & Shuttleworth, Lincoln; Hooper, London; March, Jones & Cribb, Leeds; Nieuport & General Aircraft, Cricklewood; Portholme Aerodome, Huntingdon; Ruston, Proctor, Lincoln. **Power plant** One 110 hp Clerget 9Z, 130 hp Clerget 9B, 140 hp Clerget 9Bf, 110 hp or 170 hp Le Rhòne, 100 hp Gnome Monosoupape, or 150 hp Bentley BR1. **Dimensions** Span 28 ft. Length, 18 ft 9 in with Clerget and 18 ft 6 in with BR1. Height, 8 ft 6 in. **Weight** (Clerget version) Empty, 929 lb. Loaded, 1,453 lb. **Performance** Max speed, (Clerget version) 115 mph at 6,500 ft. Service ceiling 19,000 ft. **Armament** Dual fixed, synchronized Vickers machine-guns. Provision for four 25 lb bombs below wings.

This classic dog-fighting aircraft, developed as a successor to the Pup, got its name from the 'hump' over the gun breeches. The nickname 'Camel' was later officially adopted by the Royal Flying Corps. From the outset excellent manoeuvrability was all important so most of the Camel's weight (engine, fuel tanks, machine-guns, ammunition and pilot) was concentrated well forward near the centre of gravity. Its short fuselage and the high torque of the large rotary engine could easily trap the unwary pilot but in the hands of an experienced aviator it was a close rival to the Fokker DRVII.

The Fokker DRVII is generally regarded as the finest fighter of the First World War but the Camel was the most successful, destroying a record total of 2,800 enemy aircraft on the Western Front alone. The Camel first went into action with the Royal Flying Corps in July 1917 with 70 Squadron. By October 1918 the RAF had more than 2,600 Camels on charge, equipping some 32 squadrons. The type also served on the Western Front with the *Aviation Militaire Belge* and the US Air Service.

Camels also equipped ten Royal Naval Air Service squadrons which subsequently became RAF squadrons in April 1918. The RNAS Camel first saw action on 4 June 1917 during a single combat by F/Cmdr A. M. Shook. On 4 July that year five F1 Camels from the RNAS station at Dunkirk attacked a formation of Gothas returning from a raid over England. The F1 Camel served with both the RFC and the RNAS but the 2F1 was designed especially for operation as a shipboard fighter. It differed from the previous model in having tubular centre-section struts instead of wooden struts and the fuselage was constructed in two halves, the rear half being detachable to conserve space aboard ship.

Sopwith Camels of 73 Squadron RAF at a landing ground near Humieres on 6 April 1918.

Since 1914 the air defence of Great Britain was entrusted to the RNAS, until the RFC took over the responsibility again, and the main operational function of the 2F1 Camels was to intercept Zeppelins over the North Sea. As a result many Camels were carried aboard warships and flown from platforms mounted above gun turrets. The last Zeppelin to be destroyed in air combat was shot down on 10 August 1918 by Lieutenant S. D. Culley flying a 2F1 Camel from a

lighter towed out to sea by a destroyer of the Harwich Force.

By the end of the war these comparatively 'hot' aircraft were able to operate safely from the first conventional carriers of the Royal Navy. On 17 July 1918 seven 2F1's, each carrying two 50 lb bombs, flew off from the deck of HMS *Furious* and six successfully destroyed two Zeppelins during a bombing raid on the airship sheds at Tondern. By October 1918 some 129 2F1 Camels were serving in the RNAS and 112 were carried aboard Royal Navy ships. Most Naval Camel squadrons were disbanded in 1919.

A total of 5,490 Camels was built.

SPAD VII/XIII

Type Fighting scout. **Crew** Pilot only. **Manufacturers** Société pour Aviation et ses Dérivés (SPAD). Also built under licence by ACM, Bernard, Blériot, Borel, Kellner, Levasseur, Nieuport and SCAP in France and by Mann Egerton, Norwich. **Power plant** One Hispano-Suiza 8Ac 8-cylinder engine. **Dimensions** Span, 25 ft 8 in. Length, 20 ft 3½ in. Height, 7 ft. **Weight** Empty, 1,100 lb. Loaded, 1,550 lb. **Performance** (SVII) Max speed, 119 mph at 6,560 ft. Service ceiling, 18,000 ft. (SXIII), (220 hp Hispano-Suiza 8BA) Max speed, 133 mph at 6,560 ft, 126 mph at 16,400 ft. **Armament** (Spad VII) One fixed syncronized .303 in Vickers gun. (Spad XIII), two forward-firing fixed machine-guns.

Louis Béchereau designed the SPAD in 1916 around the new 150 hp Hispano-Suiza 8Ac 8-cylinder water-cooled engine. The SPAD VII flew for the first time in May that year and became one of the most famous French fighters used by the *escadrilles de chasse* (fighter squadrons) in the First World War. Large numbers also saw action with the RFC, US Army Air Service and Belgian and Italian air arms.

The most famous unit to use the SPAD was the elite *Group de Combat* No 12, which was known generically as '*Les Cicognes*' ('The Storks'). Among its ranks was *Capitaine* Georges Guynemer, of SPA3 and the second top French ace with 54 confirmed kills, who flew the Spad VII in early 1917.

In the late summer of 1917 the SPAD XIII made its appearance on the Western Front. Its high-aspect-ratio wing permitted a favourable rate of climb but the thin aerofoil and wing arrangement produced such bad gliding characteristics that pilots had to land the SPAD with engine on. Fortunately its robust construction enabled aviators to dive their machines with little worry of structural failure.

RFC units equipped with the SPAD VII did not re-equip on the new type. No 23 Squadron was the only British squadron wholly equipped with the SPAD. It was plagued by the unreliability of its Hispano-Suiza engine and after an undistinguished career 23 Squadron replaced the SXIII in May 1918 with the Sopwith Dolphin. The SVII outlived the Spad XIII in the RAF, continuing in post-war service with 72 Squadron in Palestine and Nos 30 and 63 Squadrons in Mesopotamia.

The loss of Spad XIII orders for the RFC was more than made up for by the introduction of the type into service with eleven *squadriglie* of the Italian *Aeronautica del Regio Esercito*, one Belgian squadron and sixteen squadrons of the American Army Air Service after the US entered the war in April 1917. Capitaine René Fonck, of Escadrille SPA103 of *Groupe de Combat* No 12, and the leading French ace with

A nimble fighter of its era was the Spad SVII.

75 confirmed kills, used the Spad SXIII to shoot down six aircraft each on two days in September 1918.

Other SPAD aces included Major Maggiore Baracca, CO of the 91a *Squadriglia* during the winter of 1917–18. His Spad XIII carried his famous prancing horse insignia in which his score rose to 34 confirmed victories. He was killed in June 1918 and was Italy's leading ace of the First World War.

The SPAD XIII was a favourite mount of the American contingent on the Western Front. Second Leiutenant Frank Luke Jr, of the 27th Aero Squadron, flew Spad XIII fighters to score 21 aerial victories in just seventeen days. He finished as the second top American ace to Captain Eddie Rickenbacker, last CO of 94th Aero Squadron who achieved most of his record 26 confirmed kills in a SPAD SXIII.

Third highest American scorer with seventeen confirmed kills was Major Gervais Raoul Lufbery who was killed on 19 May 1918. Born of French parents, Lufbery served with the SPA12 '*Escadrille Lafayette*' until America's entry into the war and he subsequently became CO of the 94th Aero Squadron where he flew a SPAD XIII painted with a Sioux Indian head and swastikas as his personal good luck symbol.

Although 8,472 SVIIs and SXIIIs were built, only 1,141 of these were produced by SPAD.

SUPERMARINE SPITFIRE Mk V

Type Fighter. **Crew** Pilot only. **Manufacturers** Supermarine Division of Vickers-Armstrongs Ltd, Castle Bromwich and by Westland Aircraft. **Power plant** Rolls-Royce Merlin 45/46/50/50A. **Dimensions** Span, 36 ft 10 in, (Clipped), 32 ft 2 in or 32 ft 7 in. Length, 29 ft 11 in. Height, 11 ft 5 in. **Weight** (VC) Empty, 5,100 lb. Loaded, 6,785 lb. **Performance** Max speed, 374 mph at 13,000 ft or 357 mph at 6,000 ft with clipped wings. Service ceiling 37,000 ft or 36,500 ft with clipped wings. **Armament** (VA), Eight .303 in Browning machine-guns in wings. (VB), two 20 mm Hispano-Suiza cannon and four .303 in machine-guns. (VC), Two 20 mm cannon; four .303 in Browning machine-guns or four 20 mm cannon. Provision for 500 lb bombs.

The Spitfire was the most famous aircraft ever to see service with the RAF and was the only Allied fighter to remain in continuous production throughout the Second World War. In all, 27 different marks saw service up until 1947 and total Spitfire/Seafire production reached 22,759. Numerically, the Mark V was the most important Spitfire produced with a total of 6,479.

During the Battle of Britain, Spitfires had gained a tactical advantage over *Luftwaffe* fighters hampered by close-escort duties over southern England. As the RAF turned to the offensive the Spitfire V was developed to enable Fighter Command to retain its initiative over the Messerschmitt Bf 109. Intended initially as a stop-gap, the Mk V was basically a Mk I or II structurally strengthened to accommodate the heavier and more powerful Rolls-Royce 1,470 hp Merlin 45 vee-12 engine. Another important difference between the Mk II and the Mk V was the introduction of metal ailerons over the former's fabric type. Rate of roll at high speeds was doubled.

The Mark VA still carried eight .303 in. Browning machine-guns but the VB housed two 20 mm cannon and four machine-guns. The Mark VC introduced a 'universal' wing capable of housing eight machine-guns, or two cannon and four machine-guns, or four cannon. Alternatively, a drop tank or 500 lb bomb could be carried under the centre fuselage.

Spitfire VAs entered service with 92 Squadron at Biggin Hill in February 1941. On 11 May 1941 the Bf 109F made its first appearance over England and one was shot down over Kent by a 91 Squadron pilot flying a Spitfire VB from Hawkinge. The Mk V ultimately equipped no less than 71 UK-based squadrons of the RAF.

The Mk VA and VB also equipped the three American 'Eagle' Squadrons in Britain. After America entered the war Spitfires were made available on 'Reverse-Lend-Lease' to equip the 31st and 52nd

Fighter Groups of the 8th Air Force in England (later embarked on an aircraft carrier and flown off to participate in the 'Torch' landings in North Africa where they continued to serve using tropicalized and cannon armed Mk Vs). In September 1942 the three 'Eagle' squadrons and their Spitfire Vs were transferred to the specially activated 4th Fighter Group at Debden, Essex. The Debden 'Eagles' retained their Mk Vs until conversion to the P-47C in March 1943.

In the RAF, about 180 Mk Is and Mk IIs were converted to Mk V standard and joined Mk Vs on daylight 'tip and run' raids, known as 'Rhubarbs', over enemy-occupied Europe during 1941–42. Spitfires would take advantage of low cloud and poor visibility to cross the enemy coast and let down to strike at targets of opportunity. These low-level sweeps were often dangerous to RAF pilots and the RAF switched to higher altitudes. At first the *Luftwaffe* ignored these high-flying incursions over the Pas de Calais so 'Circus' operations were introduced, whereby upwards of twelve squadrons of Spitfires escorted a few Blenheim bombers to short-range targets in France to lure the *Luftwaffe* into combat.

The Spitfire was intended for service overseas in dry and dusty climates so early in 1942 an effective carburettor air intake system was developed and tested by the A&AAE at Boscombe Down. Unfortunately, the tropical filter reduced the Mk V's speed by 8 mph and rate of climb by about 550 ft per minute. On 7 March 1942 the Mk V became the first Spitfire variant to serve overseas when 15 tropicalized Spitfire VBs, each fitted with a 90-gallon 'slipper' tank, were flown off 600 miles to Malta from the deck of the aircraft-carrier *Eagle*. Sixteen more were delivered by this method and during April and May 1942 the USS *Wasp* delivered a further 111 Spitfire VC's to Malta to help turn the tide of battle in this Mediterranean outpost.

By late August 1942 three RAF squadrons were equipped with the Mark V in North Africa. The Western Desert posed special problems for even the tropicalized Spitfire. The OCU at Fayid, Egypt, fitted their own simplified tropical filter, developed at the RAF MU at Aboukir and known as the 'Aboukir Filter'. In all, 24 squadrons of the RAF were equipped with the Mk V in the Middle East.

In February 1943 Spitfire Vs operating with 54 Squadron defended Darwin, Australia from Japanese attack. In October that year Spitfire Vs began operations in Burma. Altogether, four squadrons in the Far East were equipped with Spitfire Vs.

In Europe the Spitfire V's ascendancy over the *Luftwaffe* largely continued until the autumn of 1941 when the Focke Wulf 190A burst onto the scene over the coast of France. This German fighter was

Spitfire MkV of the 31st Fighter Group, 309th Squadron, Merston, Sussex, 15 March 1943 (USAF).

undoubtably the most advanced in the world and completely out-classed the Spitfire V except that the latter aircraft had a much better turning circle. Fortunately, the *Luftwaffe* failed to press home its new-found advantage, choosing to remain mainly on the defensive in the west in 1942.

Spitfire Vs had their wings clipped in an attempt to improve on the gap in performance. Trials carried out by the Air Fighting Development Unit at Duxford late in 1942 showed that the removal of the V's metal wingtips considerably improved the type's rate of roll. It also improved acceleration, speed and dive characteristics below 10,000 ft.

A further improvement in low altitude performance was gained when the Mk V was fitted with a Merlin 50M engine. This was similar to the Merlin 45 but had a 'cropped' supercharger impeller as well as a diaphragm carburettor (in December 1941 the Mk V had become the first of the Spitfires to use a successful diaphragm carburettor to prevent engine cut out during manouevres which imposed negative-G on the aircraft). Together, the low altitude rated Merlin and clipped wing combination was designated Spitfire LF V. The eventual solution to the problem was the two-speed, two-stage-supercharged Merlin 61 which was originally designed for bombers. This engine was fitted to the Spitfire IX.

Spitfire Vs operated with several foreign air forces, including those of Portugal, Turkey, Italy, Yugoslavia, Egypt and Russia. A total of 94 Spitfire VAs were built, followed by 3,923 VBs and 2,447 VCs.

VOUGHT F4U CORSAIR

Type Carrier-borne or land-based fighter/fighter-bomber. **Crew** Pilot only.
Manufacturers Vought-Sikorsky Division, United Aircraft Corporation, Strat-
ford, Connecticut; Chance Vought Division, United Aircraft Corporation (later
Chance Vought Aircraft Incorporated), Dallas, Texas; Brewster Aeronautical
Corporation, Long Island City, New York; Goodyear Aircraft Corporation,
Akron, Ohio. **Specification (F4U-5N) — Power plant** 2,300 hp Pratt &
Whitney Double Wasp R-2800-32W. **Dimensions** Span, 41 ft. Length, 33 ft 6
in. Height, 14 ft 9 in. **Weight** Empty, 9,683 lb. Loaded, 14,106 lb. **Performance**
Max speed, 470 mph at 26,800 ft; Cruising speed, 227 mph, service ceiling,
41,400 ft. Range, 1,120 miles. **Armament** Four 20 mm machine-guns; two
1,000 lb bombs.

By far the finest carrier-borne fighter of the Second World War, the
Corsair, or 'Whistling Death' as the Japanese called it, was the first US
Navy fighter to exceed 400 mph in level flight. Of all the fighters built
during World War Two the F4U was to remain in production the
longest (until December 1952). Among its other many claims to fame
was its 11:1 ratio of kills to losses in combat against Japanese aircraft.
  The XF4U-1 flew for the first time on 29 May 1940 and the
production model appeared in June 1942. Its far-aft cockpit and
inverted gull wings represented an unorthodox design but its greatest
attribute was its excellent overall performance which was achieved
by simply designing the smallest possible airframe around the most
powerful engine. However, deck landing trials with the US Navy
revealed that the F-4U's long nose ahead of the cockpit made it
difficult for pilots to see the landing signal officer (LSO). For this reason
the first F-4Us were used as land-based fighters. Deliveries of the
F4U-I to the US Marine Corps began in October 1942 and the type
was first used in action by the 'Cactus Air Force' during the defence
of Guadalcanal from Japanese air, ground and sea assaults in
February 1943.
  It was not until 1944 that the F-4U was finally deemed ready for
carrier-based operations. Improvements to the cockpit included a
raised pilot's seat and a large single-piece canopy, while pilots
perfected a new landing approach, often with their port wing slightly
down so that the LSO could be kept in sight.
  The Fleet Air Arm were the first to use Corsairs at sea, on 3 April
1944, when British carrier-borne aircraft attacked the German
battleship *Tirpitz*. On this occasion the Corsairs were embarked in
HMS *Victorious* with 1834 Squadron. During July 1944 Corsairs of
1841 Squadron embarked in HMS *Formidable* provided fighter cover

Corsair II of 1830 Squadron, Fleet Air Arm (Charles E. Brown).

for further attacks on the *Tirpitz* and were joined by 1842 Squadron in the last strikes during August 1944.

Corsair F4U-4 and -5s were supplied to Britain under Lend-Lease and designated Mark I and II respectively. The Corsair II differed from the Mark I in having improved-visibility cockpit canopies and clipped wings (of 16 inches less span) to facilitate below deck storage in British carriers. The Corsair II also introduced points for the mounting of a 2,000 lb bomb or additional long-range fuel tanks. By the end of 1943 the Corsair Mk I and II equipped eight squadrons of the Fleet Air Arm.

The F-4U fought in every major Pacific battle with the US Navy, flying 64,051 sorties and destroying 2,140 Japanese aircraft with the loss of only 189 of its number. One of the most remarkable kills of the war occurred during the battle for Okinawa. Lieutenant Robert Klingman pursued a Japanese 'Nick' to 38,000 ft and brought it down by sawing off its rudder and elevators with his propeller after his machine-guns had frozen.

From 19 April 1944 FAA Corsairs also gave sterling service in the Pacific, including the historic attacks on the Palembang oil refineries

F4U-I Corsair of VF-17. This heavily weathered example was the personal steed of Ira Kepford, who eventually chalked up some seventeen victories in combat in World War 2 (USAF).

on 24 and 29 January 1945 when they destroyed thirteen Japanese fighters. During the period 26 March to 14 April 1945 1830 and 1833 Squadrons flew almost 400 of the 2,000 sorties flown from the four carriers of the British Pacific Fleet. Between 17 July and 10 August 1945 four squadrons of FAA Corsairs embarked in HMS *Victorious* and *Formidable* made a series of raids in the Tokyo area. During this period, on 9 August, Lieutenant R. H. Gray of the Royal Canadian Volunteer Reserve won a posthumous VC for his leadership during a raid on Shiogame.

By April 1945 the Corsair equipped nineteen squadrons of the Fleet Air Arm. By the end of the Pacific war only four Corsair squadrons were still in service and the last of these, Nos 1831 and 1851, remained operational until August 1946.

Although production ceased in December 1952 after 12,571 had been built, the F4U saw action in the Korean War 1950–53. It was during this conflict that a Corsair was credited with the destruction of a MiG-15 jet. The F4U finally ended its US Marine Corps career in 1954, seeing service in the Korean War as the AU-1 ground attack aircraft. It also saw action in Indo-China with the French *Aéronavale*, who used the Corsair until 1965.

YAKOVLEV YAK-1/3

Type Fighter. **Crew** Pilot only. **Manufacturers** The design bureau of A. S. Yakovlev. **Power plant** (1M) One Klimov VK-105PF. (-3) One VK-105PF-2. **Dimensions** Span, 30 ft 2¼ in. Length, 27 ft 10 ¼ in. Height, 7 ft 10 in. **Weight** Empty, 4,960 lb. Loaded, 5,864 lb. **Performance** Max speed, 404 mph. Service ceiling, 35,450 ft. **Armament** One 20 mm ShVAK cannon fired through propeller hub and two wing-mounted 12.7 mm BS machine-guns. Provision for six RS-82 rockets.

Experience gained in the Spanish Civil War prompted the Soviet Union in 1939–40 to develop new figher prototypes like the Yak-1, MiG-I and LaGG-3. Alexander S. Yakovlev is reputed to have based his extremely successful Yak-1 design on the Supermarine Spitfire and Bf 109. It was his first fighter design and the type made its first public appearance during an air display on 7 November 1940. The Yak-1 beat three other rival prototypes and production began in June 1941.

Soviet fighter specifications of the time were mindful of a ground support role and of the fact that the type would have to operate over

Early Yak 3 of the Soviet Air Force (Novosti).

vast territories away from industrial centres, often in appalling weather conditions. The Soviet climate was largely responsible for the Yak's robust construction. It had to be strong, yet light enough to land and take off from hard rolled earth or snowpacked surfaces and its equipment had to be simple to maintain.

Cockpit protection was afforded by armoured glass which took the place of armour plate around the pilot's shoulder height. The cockpit was so roomy that a pilot could turn completely in all directions including 180° aft. He could see the extent of his fuel supply by reading the gauges, which on the Yak were located on the wings! Another strange invention was the Yak's ability to receive burnt gases via a filter back into the emptying fuel tank in flight.

In the face of German advances, Yakovlev had to move his assembly lines from Klimki to near Moscow 1,000 miles distant. However, production was delayed for only six weeks and approximately 500 Yak-1s were in action against the *Luftwaffe* by the end of 1941. The Yak-1M replaced the Yak-1 on the production lines in 1942 and further improvements late in December 1942 led to the Yak-3. This type was first delivered to units in the summer of 1943. To its cost the *Luftwaffe* discovered that the Yak-3 was superior to the Bf 109G below 19,685 ft and it could turn inside the FW190 fighter-bomber. One of the new units to receive the Yak-3 was the French Regiment *Normandie-Niemen*, which had served in the Soviet Air Force since February 1943.

The final version of the Yak-3 was the 3U, powered by the 1,700 hp VK-107A. It had a top speed of 447 mph at 18,865 ft and was armed with three cannon. Although it entered production in late 1944 it did not reach first-line units until after hostilities had ended. On 1 May 1945 three Yak-3 fighters flew low over crumbling Berlin and dropped a red banner over the Reichstag proclaiming victory in the war against the Third Reich.

Altogether, some 37,000 Yak-1, -3, -7 and -9 fighters were built.

INDEX